Rooftop
Gardening

Rooftop Gardening

Kathleen Cronin Tinkel

CHILTON BOOK COMPANY
Radnor, Pennsylvania

Published in Radnor, Pa., by Chilton Book Company and simultaneously in Don Mills, Ontario,
Canada, by Thomas Nelson & Sons, Ltd.
All black and white and color photographs by Jack Tinkel

Designed by Anne Churchman

Manufactured in the United States of America

Library of Congress Cataloging in Publication Data
Tinkel, Kathleen Cronin.
  Rooftop gardening.

  Bibliography: p. 127
  Includes index.
  1. Roof gardening. I. Title.
SB419.5.T56   635.9'671   77-6145
ISBN 0-8019-6460-1
ISBN 0-8019-6461-X pbk.

1 2 3 4 5 6 7 8 9 0   5 4 3 2 1 0 9 8 7

Acknowledgments

I know of no way a person working entirely alone can write a book, and this is no exception. I am grateful to many people who helped through the months of researching, writing and photographing, especially my husband, Jack, who took most of the pictures and tolerated me during all the highs and lows of the project. I appreciate the invaluable assistance of Chris Beecher, an NYU biology graduate student who read parts of the text for technical accuracy; of Kerrie Jacks, who read parts for style and consistency; and of Lowell Nesbitt, Leslie Ray, Bill and Margaret Browne, and the New Hampshire native in SoHo, along with others who allowed us to work on their roofs. Karen Jacobus, now director of the Garden Shop at the Brooklyn Botanical Garden, and Carolyn Busch offered wonderful encouragement, help, and the use of their library when they were running Greenleaves plant store in SoHo. I also thank Karen, along with Richard Becker, for providing additional photographs. I am grateful to Craig and Alexa Pierce, who started the whole thing one evening at the dog run, and other neighbors, friends, and dog runners—Kip and Judy Coburn, Charles Leslie, Fritz Lohman, Mike and Rena Mueller, Ilene Waxler, to name a few—who encouraged me and helped me follow through. None of these people is responsible, of course, for any error I may have perpetrated.

Contents

Introduction
How to Use This Book

More information on gardening than on any other popular subject is released every year. There must be at least as many plant catalogs as all other types of catalogs, and as many gardening gadgets as kitchen gadgets—and that's a lot. Organizing the relevant material became the major problem of writing this book. Other difficulties concerned limiting the subject usefully, dragging interpretations of building and other municipal codes out of various New York City agencies and avoiding folkloric versions of botany and horticulture. To achieve this, the manuscript has been read in whole or in part by a botanist, a horticulturist, a plant store owner, a physicist (my husband), an attorney, an engineer, and a landscape designer, as well as several avid in-city gardeners of varied inclinations and views. While I hardly expected a consensus, I feel certain that this book presents a relevant version of the truth and that it will help people to garden on their roofs.

Rooftop Gardening is designed to be read months before you begin, to allow for planning and preparation of the garden. Consequently, it begins by discussing sources of gardening information and by defining potential legal and regulatory difficulties, even though these vary from place to place. I use New York not only because I live here, but also because this is one of the most tortuous cities to do anything in, and few other cities could present any more problems. The book moves to the roof itself, then to plants and gardening in general. Discussion follows on plant selection and specific roof-gardening practice. The sources, publications, distributors, and associations listed here are selective but for the most part not reviewed; they are simply those which have been useful to me or with which I am familiar. There are others which I have simply not explored.

1

Every Roof Should
Have a Garden

A garden on every roof? That's a favorite day-dream of mine; one that finally looks as if it might come true. People have gardened on their roofs since they started living in cities, but never and nowhere else have there been so many roof gar-

dens as in America today. Until recently, city gardens were usually on the terraces and around the penthouses of the rich. They were planted in hedges with a few formal flowers for the spring and tended by professionals who came in twice a

These older, relatively formal buildings seem to have influenced the gardeners working on them, but the result is harmonious if not exciting.

City roofs come in many styles and conditions. This one, which looks so unpromising, actually became an excellent roof garden. This view is toward the south, but there are no obstructions on the other sides either.

Another group of older city roofs, all good sites for gardening.

week. Today's gardens are different. They are on roofs or, in desperate cases, on fire escapes; they are as likely to feature food as flowers; and they're tended by their owners. Even the gardens of the rich are changing. The well-known New York philanthropist, Stewart Mott, feeds his family and staff from his Park Avenue penthouse garden. City governments—which have in the past seemed to thrive on raising objections to any project even remotely unorthodox—are turning around and encouraging city dwellers to use the roofs of multistory buildings. In New York, the City Planning Commission has stipulated that certain new apartment houses be built with roof gardens covering a portion of the roofs and seems ready to encourage gardens and other roof facilities for residents in renovated buildings as well. Who knows—we may yet see blocks of living, green-topped city roofs.

The merits of roof gardens are obvious: more city gardeners have access to roofs than to plots of land. Furthermore, most roofs are preferable to the typical abused and dark city lot or tiny window box. Even if you have a classical high-pressure,

no-free-time, big-city life style, the soothing release of gardening can be just a few steps (or an elevator ride) away. Roof gardens bring the fruits of your labors right to your home where they are easy to harvest; meanwhile, relaxing in a garden in the middle of the city is luxury without a price. Among the horticultural advantages, soil in rooftop containers usually warms up earlier and stays warm later in the season than soil in the ground, enabling Northern gardeners to extend the growing season somewhat. This characteristic also enables roof gardeners to grow tender plants, which would normally be hardy only farther south. Perhaps because there is more wind at roof level, or because roofs rise above traffic and most industry, roof gardens often receive less noise, soot, smoke, exhaust, and other pollution than gardens on the ground just below them; and the sun is usually stronger, as it is less obstructed.

Roofs, however, are neither yards nor shelves in a south-facing window. The same characteristics which help roof gardens—warmth, strong sun, and wind—can create problems as well, although few roofs are so hot, stormy, sunny, or windy (or

More city roofs, these blocked to both the south and west by taller buildings, yet very suitable for shrubs and other plants which don't need long days of direct sun.

small, crowded, or weak, for that matter) that they cannot support a garden of some sort. A dedicated gardener can have a garden on any roof, although you will need more determination for gardening on the roof than for growing traditional houseplants or a few herbs in a window box. Some of the most exciting and productive city gardens have been created against incredible odds: in nearly lightless and airless "air" shafts, on minuscule balconies without sun or without shade, among service structures on old tenements or modern concrete rooftops, suspended around fire escapes or perched on windowsills. It is commonly held that art is the overcoming of limitations—so is roof gardening. And, in both cases, the rewards are great.

Today's gardening is a personal activity, often performed as much for recreation or pleasure as for produce, and roof gardens can have nearly as many styles as the people who make them. They can be formal or casual; used primarily for ornamental or for edible plants; or designed for summers only or for year-round use. They can be professionally designed, planted, and maintained or entirely homemade. Roof gardening combines the best of houseplant and outdoor gardening: it combines the more or less natural growing conditions of outdoors—full sun, a relatively large space, natural pollinization, and the schedule of light and dark to which plants have adapted—with all the advantages of home—accessibility, freedom from many pests and diseases, access to water and the control of other cultural necessities, such as soil, fertilizers, humidity, and wind. Plants too large and unwieldy for your living room but too delicate for the back yard can be grown beautifully on the roof, where a container which loomed awkwardly indoors will seem well proportioned and graceful.

These are typical small tenement roofs, full of stacks, outbuildings, and other immovable structures.

"EXPERIENCE KEEPS A DEAR SCHOOL . . ."
—LEARNING ABOUT PLANTS

Observation and experience are great teachers, but they do not provide good answers to every gardening question. The subject is too large. Some aspects of growth are so complex they seem to be magical rather than rational and logical. Probably because of this gardeners sometimes tend to look for outrageous explanations or, conversely, to take refuge in the obvious, though neither approach works for the long run. In fact, though the anatomy and physiology of plants are nearly as complex as the related studies of animals, anyone interested in gardening can learn their essentials, and should. Plants communicate, sometimes dramatically, by wilting, shooting up floppy stems, dropping buds, or making excessively lush foliage, for example. If you learn their language, you can understand them. You could achieve this understanding through experience alone, of course, but losing plants can be expensive—and that's often what is meant by the expression "learning by experience." While it is one thing to read about growth and quite another to ensure it, reading is the most readily available, up-to-date, and reliable source of gardening information. Since this book is clearly neither an encyclopedia nor a textbook, it is meant to be used with other sources of information. The amount of information printed on gardening subjects is staggering. Government agencies, businesses involved in agriculture, state agricultural colleges, and state and federal experiment stations produce information literally faster than one can read it. Much of this is primary material, but it wends its way into books, magazines, and newspapers, making them interesting and useful reading for every gardener. Some of these publications include *Horticulture, Organic Farming & Gardening, The Avant Gardener* and *Blair & Ketchum's Country Journal,* but the bulletins of botanical gardens and arboreta are also helpful, as are Sunday newspaper gardening sections.

If in addition to strictly horticultural wisdom you are seeking inspiration, you should take a trip to the nearest botanical garden. Public gardens are not necessarily a surefire source of specific infor-mation about what will grow well in your garden. After all, botanical gardens usually employ highly trained professionals for whom horticulture is a full-time occupation, and they have the newest equipment and up-to-date methods; why shouldn't plants grow for them? However, botanical gardens do stimulate the mind's eye. They are beautifully laid out, with graceful arrangements of thriving trees, shrubs, ground covers, foliage, blossoms, ponds, walkways, and small buildings.

One of the best sources of down-to-earth gardening advice is a good local nursery or serious plant store. First of all, you can see at first hand the wide variety of plants, tools, and containers available, and their cost. Secondly, the plants sold in such a store probably represent what people are actually growing (for whatever reason) this year in all sorts of gardens, even if they may not include all the plants that will grow on your roof. Many nurseries are run by dedicated plant "nuts" who, in their own way, have as rich and reliable a collection of horticultural wisdom as many academic botanists. They are the best source of information on the installation, care, and growth habits of the plants they sell, since their knowledge comes from practical experience acquired by caring for the plants they sell and the gardens they maintain.

One of the best bargains in large cities, and increasingly in smaller ones, is the free or nominally priced on-site consultation offered by plant store or nursery garden designers who will analyze your roof for typical and atypical features, strong points and weaknesses, and give you a design scaled to your garden ideas and your budget. In many shops, the fee is credited to later purchases. It is often worth the small amount charged, even if it is not later credited, just for access to the accumulated wisdom of such a designer, particularly if your roof is difficult to reach, oddly shaped, or very shady or windy. What is obvious to a professional might take considerable time and trouble, even trial and error, for you to see and accomplish.

If you love life in the city—or need to be there for some reason—but wish you, like your cousins in the suburbs, could have a real garden, the roof may be your answer. Roof gardening is so exciting and so satisfying, in fact, that you may very well choose never to give it up, no matter how many "real" gardens you acquire. Meanwhile, though no one can beat nature, you can probably strike an excellent bargain with it on your roof.

IT PAYS TO AVOID LEGAL PROBLEMS

In virtually every city there are ordinances which directly or indirectly restrict the use of roofs. Sometimes different agencies have overlapping responsibilities and seemingly contradictory regulations. Sometimes these are difficult to interpret. While municipal codes usually do not prohibit a roof garden explicitly, they often say that you cannot place a fence on a roof between adjoining buildings, or that you cannot have "obstructions" on the roof, and inspectors may view planters, furniture, trellises, and hoses, for example, as obstructions. Building safety codes may prohibit placing heavy objects, planters for instance, along parapets where they can fall off (even if you think they are safe) or having water or soil on the roof because they can blow around and become a nuisance to your neighbors. Other codes may state that you cannot build or place anything beyond the building lot line, such as window boxes, hanging planters, or window greenhouses, although inspectors often seem to overlook small window boxes (not to mention window air conditioners) in enforcing these codes. You are likely to need a license to attach anything (a workshed, for instance) to your roof, or to construct anything more sizable than a few benches or shelves. The fire department may have regulations intended to maintain access from building to roof and from building to building via the roofs. Fire or insurance regulations may restrict you from placing any object within a specific number of feet from an exit, wall, or fire escape. Inflammable materials, such as wood, straw, bamboo, or certain plastics, may be forbidden on the roof as fire hazards; or towns in drought areas may require that fences, decks, garden fixtures, and even mulches be fireproofed, which may make using these traditional materials expensive if not impossible. Blocking or crowding skylights may violate building codes, since they were probably placed to give an interior room its required minimum of light and air.

On the other hand, some municipalities actually require that roofs in new constructions and reno-

Small greenhouses are most convenient when placed on a terrace, but the new small models are also adaptable to roofs. Check local regulations before buying, however.

vations be available to residents. Where developers have taken land that was once used by the public to build multistory office or apartment complexes, city planners impose the requirement to return something to the people whose open space has disappeared. Independent builders can request variances so they can include the roof legally as an extension of living space for their tenants, thereby improving their sales position without violating city height limitations. In New York, Boston, and perhaps other cities, a quiet movement is growing to open roofs to apartment dwellers if they are or can be made safe enough to satisfy insurance underwriter and bureaucratic regulations, and to require that new buildings have safe, usable roofs. Whether all this newly exposed space becomes gardens or some other recreational facility is another question entirely, but it is certainly one which city residents should help to determine. Decisions regarding building use, public safety, and planning are made by such agencies as planning and zoning commissions, buildings departments, and boards of standards and appeals. (Names of agencies vary but are listed in your telephone directory, under ''Town Name—Government of,'' or can be located through city information services.)

Landlord—If you are a tenant you need your landlord's permission to use the roof, since this privilege is not generally included, and may be explicitly forbidden, in standard leases. It may be necessary and advantageous for both you and your landlord to make special contractual arrangements for use of the roof. You should at least have a general agreement in writing, including a detailed description of the present condition of the roof, since any damage, even that normally attributed to its age, material, and method of construction, may become ''your fault,'' and you may end up having to make repairs whether or not your garden has actually caused the damage and, more to the point, whether or not someone can prove that it has. On the other hand, in fairness to your landlord, badly designed or maintained roof gardens can damage the roof and the floors beneath it. Your landlord is entitled to expect you to protect the roof against unreasonable damage.

Likely problem areas include the roof surface which, since it was designed for fast runoff of water, may not stand up well to gardening conditions of constant moisture, regular foot traffic, and heavy immobile containers. In terms of plain strength, roofs are not necessarily braced like the floors below them, but in Northern areas, at least, they have been built to withstand the considerable weight of accumulated snow. Gutters and downspouts are not normally designed to take the amounts of debris produced by gardening and can back up unless you supplement existing drains or, at least, screen the opening before you bring in plants. Running hoses up along exterior walls may cause water to drip on passersby, on your neighbor's terrace, or on other parts of the building, making surfaces slippery and sometimes discoloring masonry or metal walls. And if plants are allowed to drain on parapets or ledges of the building, fertilizer deposits may build up, causing stains or even mossy growths which may be unsightly and hard to remove, if not actually damaging to the building.

You can protect yourself from these unplanned and unwelcome fruits of roof gardening by outlining specific areas of responsibility in advance with your landlord, in writing if possible, and by exercising ordinary common sense in planning and maintaining your garden.

Neighbors—Besides the strictly legal problems which concern you and your landlord, there are other general regulations designed to protect the public. These codes may forbid cooking outdoors, for example, or prohibit noise, livestock, compost piles, or any object which blocks your neighbor's view or fresh air. Information about relevant codes and their enforcement is available from your police station or from other city agencies.

Any discussion of regulations governing the use of roofs must include the unwritten laws of courtesy and fair play. While there is probably no specific law on the books forbidding you from letting water, smoke, or sprays land on your neighbor's laundry (or on your neighbor, for that matter), common sense, common courtesy, or the golden rule may develop the force of law.

Agricultural regulatory agencies—There are also many city, county, state, or federal agricultural regulations controlling some species and varieties of plants. Certain fruits cannot be brought into California, for instance, and protected varieties of many plants cannot be removed from some areas. These regulations are designed to control the spread of agricultural diseases or pests, to prevent threatened varieties from foragers, or to prevent certain plants from becoming rampant. Because roofs are small and seem safely isolated, it is tempting to ignore these and other agricultural regulations on the premise that just one specimen can make no difference. But even roof gardens have visitations of strange weeds and insects, apparently out of nowhere, which help to explain why the regulations exist; plants and plant pests have phenomenal transportation systems, and it is worse than foolish to take a chance. Agricultural regulations are binding on gardeners everywhere, as part of a large-scale attempt to prevent major epidemics, like the Dutch elm disease, which may threaten entire species of plants. You can find out about local restrictions, and get good gardening advice as well, from local agricultural agencies (listed under "City, County, or State Name or United States—Government of" in the telephone directory), your state's land grant college, or county extension agent. Many of these sources are listed in the back of this book.

2

Turning Your Roof
Into a Garden

A city has a roof terrain just as it has a more obvious terrain at street level. A view across the roofs is as varied in shape, height, and texture as any other city scene, with the added benefit of a second view of the busy world below. Roof views nourish fantasy: water towers rise like motley minarets. Parapets appear to be shallow medieval forts, guarding empty territories. Moon and sun-thrown shadows dramatize smokestacks, ventilators, funnels, pillars, and odd devices which rise like ritual statues of some old society. But fantasies shift as gardeners move to the roofs. Yesterday's oases are today's (or at least tomorrow's) groves, as lonely trees and random gardens are replaced with whole rooftops of green.

MAKING PLANS

Like most transitions from fantasy to reality, converting tar beach to paradise will take planning as well as physical work. To most people, nothing sounds more boring than making formal plans, but, in fact, planning brings dreams into focus, and good useful roof garden plans can be very simple and even fun to do. Meanwhile, plans will help you avoid such expensive pitfalls as overbuying or choosing inappropriate plants for the conditions on your roof. Furthermore, a set of plans can help you win the landlord's approval for your roof garden. Unless you are one of those fortunate people with a comprehensive mental image of your garden-to-be, however, you will have to de-

velop your garden plans one step at a time. Before you so much as open a seed catalog, or make a mark on paper, go up to your roof. Take along a pad and pencil, white chalk (or a stick, if there is snow on the roof), and a measuring tool, preferably a steel tape measure, or a folding carpenter's rule. Walk around the roof a little, getting a feel for the space. Try to visualize different gardening areas and to decide where you would be most comfortable sitting, working, or looking. Mark these areas out on the roof surface. Include spaces for working, sitting, planting shrubs, vines, tall plants, flowers or vegetables. Obviously, these choices may change later as you have more information on such crucial things as how the sun moves over your garden and you have arrived at a list of plants and a general diagram of your roof.

At this point you are ready to make a sketch of the roof. Draw a rectangle or square approximating the proportions of your roof and mark north or an adjoining street to avoid confusion later. Besides the dimensions of the roof, you will also need to mark the location and dimension of any roof fixture, such as an elevator housing, water tower, or ventilator. Mark parapet heights, adjoining higher walls, any windows overlooking your roof, as you should not block them, and the location of drains and any utilities such as electric outlets, light fixtures, or water supply. You should also indicate the position of permanent eyesores (particularly blinking neon lights, which can drive you crazy), street lights visible from the roof,

A Typical City Roof
(South)

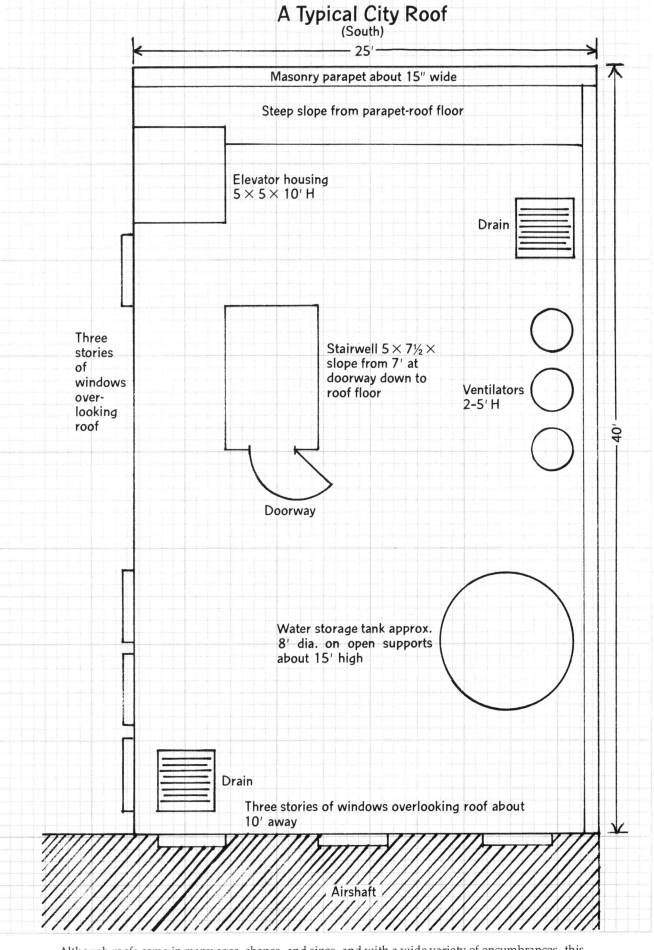

Although roofs come in many ages, shapes, and sizes, and with a wide variety of encumbrances, this drawing illustrates a fairly typical Northeastern city roof.

A Possible Garden Plan

Peas, then morning glories, trained on nets; wood planters
4 × 1 × 1' deep.

Workbench,
shelves
and sink.

Entire area from east side past stairwell decked. Large
ell shaded with split bamboo screens stretched across
2 × 4" wooden uprights and cross braces.

Hose
pulled
up from
apart-
ment
below.

Vegetables and annuals in
various containers.

Houseplants summering
under and around water
storage tank.

The easiest way to make a roof garden is to use existing structures for shade and support. This drawing shows a relatively simple garden built on the roof shown in the previous drawing. This garden cost very little to set up. If the deck and screened area were eliminated, it would have cost even less, though it would also limit the plants that would grow well there.

billboards, a constant (or regular) noise source, or any other form of pollution you may want to block. If the sun is visible, indicate its pattern, even though it will shift from season to season, and find the prevalent wind direction by holding a strip of paper and watching how it bends or drifts. Mark this on your drawing, as well as any areas on your roof where there is noticeable turbulence.

When you come inside, you can redraw, using graph paper (ruled 4 or 8 to the inch, in light blue or green ink), which makes drawing the roof and its details to scale rather easy. Then, by slipping the drawing of the roof under a sheet of tracing paper, you can sketch in tentative garden plans. Because of the grid, you can use accurate proportions, to ensure that you actually have all the space you think you have. (When arranging space without a drawing—usually just before falling asleep or standing in the shower—I always seem to have twice as much room as actually exists. Things I visualized as being surrounded by open space end up crowded together; some things don't fit at all. Using graph paper can help you avoid some of these problems.) While locating large facilities— such as a deck, work area, or row of large plants for screening—may be best accomplished on the roof itself where the complex considerations affecting your decision are present and obvious, the details and the interrelationships of one garden unit with another—such as supplying water and drains to a potting bench and a recreation area at the same time—are best worked out on paper.

The garden you design, first on paper and then on your roof, can take many forms and styles, from casual/functional to ornate/showy. How it turns out depends not only on your taste but also on other factors such as cost; amount and type of space available; legal (or landlord) restrictions on your use of the roof; suitability of the roof for gardening without modification; the plants you want to grow—vegetables, fruits, flowers, shrubs, trees, vines, even water plants or tropical specialties, and the relative amounts of space you want to allot to each; the facilities you intend to have in your garden, from a simple workbench to a screened deck, lath house or even a greenhouse or other more elaborate structure, and whether you are free to build permanently on the roof or must restrict

your plans to portable units; the equipment necessary to offset a poor gardening climate or pollution.

If there is any simple watchword for planning a roof garden, it is this: go slowly. It is not only expensive but somehow immoral to destroy plants because they were chosen too hastily or planted in the wrong container or in the wrong garden altogether.

PREPARING THE SURFACE

Creating even a very simple garden on the average roof will require some preparation. While most roofs are good at their primary function of protecting the building, few have been designed and built especially for gardening. The tar paper/asphalt roofs so common on older buildings in the Northeast, for instance, can go for years without leaking, through storms, heavy snow, freezing in the winter and baking in summer sun. But those same roofs often cannot take the daily walking, frequent watering, and heavy containers needed for gardening, at least not without modification. On the other hand, modern poured concrete buildings are structurally well suited for gardening, but the surface may glare, bounce noise around, be dangerously slippery when wet, or even just too "cold looking" for a garden. In fact, most roofs are dangerous and/or downright ugly, unsuitable for people and for plants, and it is your problem as a roof gardener to correct this situation.

There are many approaches to creating a garden on the roof, however. You can emphasize function, or appearance, plan for one season or ten and for one type of plant or a variety. Certainly you can accomplish any of these extravagantly or on a modest budget. While a lack of money may limit the details of your garden, the exercise of taste and energy will guarantee you the substance.

There are many materials for covering all or part of your roof surface, in every price range (or even without cost), but it is sometimes difficult to find one that fulfills all your gardening needs, which may include:

Providing air spaces beneath containers, which

will leave fewer hiding places for insects and will help to insulate the roots from the roof's heat and to give the container room to drain.

Changing the color or texture of the roof surface to reduce absorption of light and heat or to reduce glare from sunlight.

Protecting the roof surface from (and distributing the load of) foot traffic, furniture legs, and moist, heavy containers, which will prevent punctures to the surface (a problem particularly with tar paper) or even damage to the structure of the building.

Helping to retain moisture around plants, thus to increase the relative humidity of your garden.

Improving the appearance of your garden, even creating illusions of spaciousness, surface variety, or levels.

Duckboards distribute loads well. They are decorative in a rhythmical, almost Oriental way and permit excellent air circulation, especially if built openly or on high (4- to 6-inch) supports. They reflect light gently without creating glare, which can be a problem particularly in large cities. Duckboards can be built easily, using basic woodworking tools. Although new lumber is expensive, duckboards can be made of scrap, and they can be constructed in separate units light enough for a person to move. You can begin logically with a duckboard sun deck and walkways

between containers, extending gradually each season to other parts of the roof.

Loose stones, marble chips, and gravel are good functional and decorative surface coverings, at least on concrete roofs. They are excellent for helping to maintain humidity, but may actually cause surface damage on tar paper or asphalt roofs if they are used to trap moisture against the surface, or if heavy containers are allowed to rest directly on them. On a concrete, brick, or stone surface, however, they are perfectly safe, and they are useful to soften the rectangular outlines common to these types of buildings. Stones can also be swept aside easily to permit cleaning or rearranging of garden areas. With all these virtues, stones have one overriding drawback—they get filthy. Stones accumulate all sorts of debris, even up on the roof—dead leaves and stems, windborne junk like gum wrappers and cigarette butts—and, unless you sit down and pick through them by hand, they are impossible to clean, as they will clog the intake of even industrial vacuum cleaners.

Wood or bark chips are an even cheaper material, useful for roofs which are well sheltered from the wind. Chips are decorative, usually aromatic, and certainly consistent with the appearance of a garden. Their usage is limited, however, since they decompose if kept moist, and they can become dry enough, on the other hand, to create a fire hazard.

Duckboards are not only useful for protecting the roof surface but they also make dramatic visual patterns in the garden.

Depending on their origin, chips may contain insects or bacteria and, in any event, are attractive to these pests. Worst of all, no matter how little wind you believe exists, these chips just seem to disappear, and you find yourself replacing them every few weeks. Clean chips are an excellent decorative and moisture-retaining mulch for plants in containers, however. (In many cities you can have your Christmas tree processed into chips by recycling organizations.)

If your roof is noisy, or if light bounces around uncomfortably, you might consider using a *carpet* of moisture-proof, weather-proof synthetic material. There are materials which simulate (more or less successfully) woven grasses, lawns (like Astroturf), or even regular indoor carpets of almost any pattern. The first time I saw one on a roof, it looked and felt bizarre, but the materials have gradually come to seem amusing, or even appropriate. They are certainly preferable to high levels of noise and glare. Although they do not actually absorb water, these mats can trap it against the roof surface and should be lifted occasionally to air out the roof, to check its covering, and to air and, if necessary, wash the rug. Despite their thinness and flexibility, these materials protect tar paper surfaces from occasional foot traffic fairly well, as long as people are not wearing spikes. They are not a good support for plants, however. In fact, it is probably best to cut away sections of carpeting beneath containers so they can be propped up on feet or bricks. The major practical drawback of rugs is their texture, which can harbor bacteria,

insects, or insect eggs. You should look for a flat-weave rather than a shag pattern.

Sheet linoleum functions similarly—in fact, it is slightly better at distributing loads—but since it doesn't breathe, it is likely to mildew and must be aired frequently. It is probably somewhat cheaper than indoor/outdoor rugs, but it is also harder to handle, as it can crack if bent too abruptly. Depending on the color and texture, either linoleum or rugs will reflect light evenly without glare. Both are relatively easy to clean, by hosing or by washing with detergent.

If you live near a manufacturing area, you can find one of the best roof coverings, *industrial skids*, discarded in the trash. Made to load and transport heavy equipment and manufactured goods, they are well constructed, though roughly finished, and are ideal for walkways, sun decks, and plant supports. They come in many "models" which, used cleverly, are not only functional but decorative. For roof garden needs, you should look for skids with widely spaced boards to permit good air circulation and with two or three horizontal supports rather than four feet, which might dig into the roof surface. Skids are really very durable. We used them for three or four years under really dreadful conditions, before finally having to discard them because the boards were coming off the top. It is probably advisable to upend them occasionally, to make sure they are dry and not hiding any pests.

If your building and roof are stone, brick, or poured concrete it is possible to lay *bricks or stones*

Industrial skids are extremely useful for protecting roof surfaces and supporting planters.

in sand, but it is both an expensive and wasteful idea. If the roof can support all that extra weight, you should use deeper containers or more plants, not a load of sand. It is certainly a poor system for tar paper roofs, since damp sand lying against the surface may cause tears or mildew, and will certainly hide the damage. Bricks do have a place in the roof garden, however, for propping up containers to ensure good air circulation and drainage. If your roof can afford the weight, they can also be used to make a container, actually a small raised bed, for annuals or bulbs. If you want to do that, you should keep the area small, and place it near one of the building's upright supports—in a corner near a stairwell or elevator shaft, for example.

Whatever you cover the roof with, choose materials which will not harm the building structure or the roof surface. Look for a material which solves more than one gardening or aesthetic problem and which you can afford not only to make or buy but also to maintain and replace as necessary.

The roofs of modern buildings are often enclosed by waist-high walls for safety.

FENCES, RAILINGS, AND WALLS

Reasons for enclosing all or part of a roof garden may include safety, aesthetics, excessive wind, sun, or noise, the need to separate one area from another or to support vines, climbing vegetables, or flowers. Whatever the reason, virtually every roof garden ends up with at least one constructed or modified vertical structure, and the best ones are planned and prepared before bringing in the plants.

Safety is the most obvious reason for building a fence, railing, or wall. What your common sense recommends, city safety regulations may require. If there are no legal height requirements, a four-foot-high barrier is effective, though you may want six feet if you need to keep trespassers out or if there will be guests—especially children, dogs, or anyone unused to open spaces—on the roof. If it is opaque (preferably opaque but not solid, for wind-control reasons), a barrier of this height will block the horizontal view when you are seated but will permit you to see surrounding higher rooftops and landmarks. An openly woven trellis or metal mesh stretched across a frame can support climbing or delicate plants, without blocking light and air.

On the other hand, you may be able to get away with no wall at all if your windy or noisy side is sheltered by a taller building, or if all your views are breathtaking (or tolerable, at least), and privacy is assured because yours is the tallest building around. If you do decide to use a barrier for any reason, it can take a variety of forms.

For a roof with a pleasant view but only a low parapet, an *iron railing* or lightweight *open fence* will do. If the view is awful or the sides are unsafe, you may have to build a more substantial fence. Unfortunately, fence building has become expensive, with producers of lumber, metal, and synthetic materials racing each other for top prices. And, unless you own the building, you will probably not want to invest much in improving it. Fortunately, some inexpensive materials are available, and some of them can be used with minimum skills and equipment.

Probably easiest, cheapest, and certainly porta-

Old-fashioned ornamental cast-iron railings are beautiful, especially when used as a support for climbing plants.

ble is a *lightweight metal mesh (chicken wire) fence.* The material comes in rolls of different widths, gauges, and various hole shapes and sizes, and it is available from most hardware stores. Many styles are available galvanized, that is, with a plated finish which protects against rust; and some styles are also manufactured with a plastic coating, usually some shade of green especially designed for gardens. Prices vary with the gauge of the wire, density of the weave, and the width of the material. The easiest, if not the most elegant, way to use this material is to unroll it and staple or nail the edges to the parapet or to a wooden frame, either freestanding or attached to the parapet. This will provide no protection against falling, but will support climbing plants. Behaving somewhat like very heavy fabric, the material is light enough for one person to manipulate—carefully, as the ends are sharp. It has a tendency to curl, and it sags with time, however. For rigidity, you can stretch the mesh across plain or fancy wooden frames, using closely spaced uprights or a combination of

sparser uprights and diagonal braces. Chicken wire and wood panels are flexible and are easy to build, handle, and store. Such sections can be pinned together, using hinges, steel bars, or other devices every eighteen inches (but no fewer than three per side, for stability), forming a zigzag freestanding screen or a flat unit to be attached to the parapet. If you use screws instead of nails for assembly, the units can be taken apart and stored inside during the winter, thus extending their lifetime.

Fences of heavy gauge chain-link metal mesh (sometimes called cyclone or hurricane fencing) are heavier and stronger than chicken wire. The mesh is usually made in a diamond-shaped, twisted link pattern. Chain-link fences look as grim and ungardenlike as prison walls do, but if you need strength or security, they can provide it. The material is also relatively expensive, and if you use plastic or redwood slats through the links to improve its appearance or to make it opaque, the cost runs even higher. Furthermore, unlike chicken wire, chain-link fencing needs professional (or at least experienced and strong) installers, and it must usually be purchased from industrial suppliers. All this tends to make it impractical except where its characteristic strength is needed and where it can be more or less permanently installed.

There are many *other types of wire fences*, such as wire pickets (single or double), low borders (which may be enough to mark the boundaries of a garden area, protect a large shrub or tree from dogs and children, or to delineate the top of a relatively safe parapet), and medium-height lawn fencing (which is not enough for otherwise unprotected roof edges). Most of these are available in discount stores, hardware stores, and lawn and garden centers, in many grades, weights, heights, and finishes. Most can be used alone or with other materials to provide minimal indications or absolute blocking of an area. Vinyl coatings are popular, especially in white and green, but the coatings increase the cost and do not seem to add much; not only do the coatings tend to peel, but most of the colors scream their unsuitability all over the garden. Happily, the plastic is usually applied over a galvanized finish, so when it wears off you

Examples of Metal Fencing

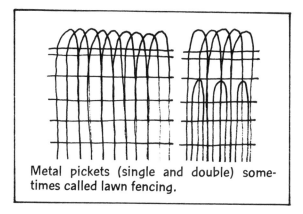

Metal pickets (single and double) sometimes called lawn fencing.

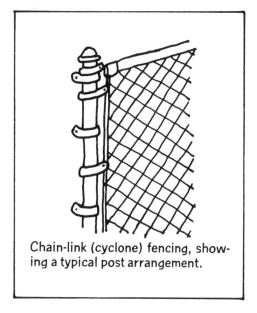

Chain-link (cyclone) fencing, showing a typical post arrangement.

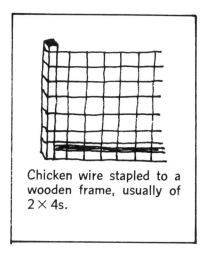

Chicken wire stapled to a wooden frame, usually of 2 × 4s.

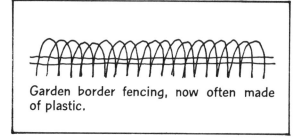

Garden border fencing, now often made of plastic.

Garden centers and hardware stores offer a wide range of metal fencing, of which five traditional forms are illustrated here. Buy galvanized steel if possible as it resists rust. It is also usually less expensive and ultimately more attractive than plastic-coated wire.

are left with what you could have bought in the first place—plain galvanized metal. Galvanized finishes mellow in a city's polluted air and recede from conscious (or, at least, glaring) view.

Today's increased interest in gardening has encouraged manufacturers to compete energetically in developing new patterns of mesh and other fences. Most companies offer free brochures on their lines, and some will send you free or nominally priced plans for using their products.

Wooden fences are also useful. They are, of course, the classical choice on the ground, but they can also be used gracefully and practically on the roof if they are scaled to the restricted small garden format, and if building and fire regulations permit their use. Wooden fences can be open or nearly opaque in pattern, simple or elegant, ready-made or custom-built, finished or rough. Wood is graceful in the garden, and it can be used in decorative patterns reflecting or contrasting

Examples of Wooden Fencing

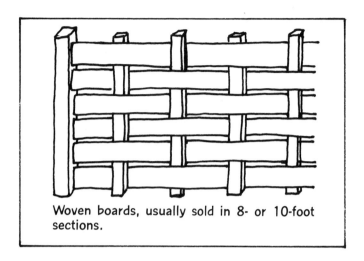

Woven boards, usually sold in 8- or 10-foot sections.

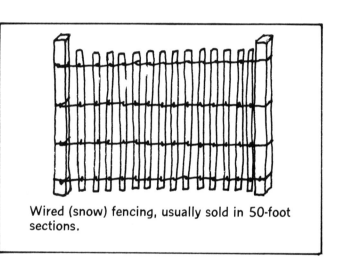

Wired (snow) fencing, usually sold in 50-foot sections.

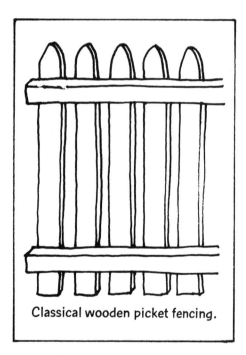

Classical wooden picket fencing.

Classical wooden fences work nicely on the roof. There are dozens of styles sold in 8- or 10-foot lengths, and many traditional patterns you can easily build yourself. This drawing illustrates three of the most common forms.

with those used for decks and containers. It is cool looking and, unless exposed to blazing direct sun for long hours, cool feeling as well. Wood may not last so long as metal but it ages more gracefully and poses fewer day-to-day problems because, unlike metal, wood neither amplifies nor retains heat, glare, and noise. Most woods can be treated to withstand moisture, or you can use the more expensive but naturally resistant woods like redwood, cedar, or cypress. However, even inexpensive woods can usually be counted on to last a few seasons without any protective finish, unless they are covered by snow all winter. All woods tend to discolor, splinter, and warp if used outdoors, even if you give them a weatherproofing treatment.

Wooden fences are particularly useful for ensuring privacy. Although completely closed fences can create more problems on a roof than they solve, a wooden fence can look opaque while it actually has openings for air to pass through. Classical designs for wooden fences include pickets, large louvers, boards mounted alternately on the fronts and backs of uprights, and woven boards. These and other designs are available ready-made through farm and garden centers, nurseries, and hardware stores, or they can be made at home with ordinary woodworking tools. Some traditional styles are cheaper ready-made than you can make them. The rolled fences of grapestakes, bamboo stalks, or wooden stakes, linked by wires, are inexpensive, portable, and have a cool orderly look. They can be simply unrolled and braced or attached to uprights or to a full frame, depending on your need for permanence or portability. Picket fences are available in lumber or molded ''wood,'' and you can get woven fences, crossed-lumber fences, and other styles in do-it-yourself kits from Sears and similar stores.

The type and grade of wood you choose will depend as much on how long you expect the fence to last and whether it will be in contact with moisture or plants as on the simple cost to buy or make it. In the West, redwood is a good choice, particularly in the economical rough or garden grade. Redwood naturally withstands typical exterior conditions, including moisture, and actually becomes more graceful as it ages. In other parts of the country, where redwood is exotic and expensive, red cedar may be available and is about as good. We have had good luck with exterior grade plywood, altogether untreated or sealed with clear polyurethane varnish. Either way, the layers tend to buckle eventually from being allowed to become wet and dry. Since fences generally are not subject to as much wear and tear, weight or persistent moisture as containers, untreated wood lasts pretty well. Incidentally, while exterior or waterproof plywood is worth extra expense, marine plywood is usually an extravagance. Both marine and waterproof plywood are laminated with waterproof glue, but marine plywood has more layers and is heavier, actually a disadvantage on a roof. Marine plywood may cost nearly twice as much as exterior-grade plywood, which costs more than standard grade.

Panels of translucent plastic or fiberglass, usually corrugated for added strength and rigidity, are increasingly popular for fences. They can be used like wood, but will obscure the view while permitting diffused light to enter your garden, a tremendous advantage for dark but too public roofs. You could use transparent panels, but the plastics scratch easily, which makes them translucent anyway, and since the clear sheets are not readily available with corrugations, you would need much heavier panels. As plastic can be hideous, especially in a garden, you need particularly good design to humanize it; framing the panels in wood or covering them with plants will help bring all but the most intransigent plastics into line, however. Here, as elsewhere, good taste and resourcefulness can triumph over ordinary (or worse) materials.

Although they are bulkier—that is, for any given effect, plants require more space than a fence does—*plants* can be used around your roof garden in lieu of a fence or railing. Plants are especially helpful in reducing noise, glare, and local air pollution. On the other hand, plants are relatively expensive, even if you plan to buy baby plants and wait until they grow up to their jobs. Plants excel as fences especially where there is widespread noise or glare. Too many plants, densely massed together, however, will make your garden seem dark and claustrophobic. They are best used along one side or another, rather than to surround the roof.

Seating areas needn't be fancy, especially when there's a delightful view!

SEATING, STORAGE, AND WORK AREAS

Gardeners often seem unwilling, in the beginning at least, to include such seeming luxuries as a shaded work and sitting area, a potting bench, or a storage shed in their roof garden plans. Everything costs so much today that it seems more logical to restrict expenditures to seeds, plants, soil components, tools, and containers, the unavoidable garden purchases. But there are often good practical reasons for taking time, energy, and money to build or buy some of these structures.

Which of them, however, and how elaborate they should be are questions with many answers. In terms of safety, a lockable storage area—even if only an old footlocker—is a necessity in most urban areas where there may be uncontrolled access to your garden. Tools, empty containers, or soil, which pose slight if any hazard on the ground, could be lethal if they were to be blown off the roof. Fertilizers, rooting hormones, pesticides (even technically nontoxic ones), and some soil-mixing ingredients may be harmful if eaten, as children, pets, or unwary guests may accidentally

A professionally mounted canvas awning shades this terrace garden's seating area.

do; so they should be locked safely away. You will also want to store expensive equipment to prevent casual borrowing or theft.

It is tiring and difficult to work on your plants without a potting bench or table, especially in the spring when large numbers of seedlings must be thinned, transplanted, and finally moved to their own containers. Even an old card table is helpful, particularly if it can be left set up and reserved for gardening purposes.

Plants need protection from the weather, and so do you when you are working or relaxing in your garden. The frame of a work or storage area is a logical support for an awning or arbor, which will shade you and some plants from direct sun during the summer. During their winter dormant cycle, many plants need protection from wind, sun, and freezing. While plants in the ground are protected by soil and by mulches built up around them, plants in containers need extra help. Grouping them in crates or sheds is one efficient and practical way to provide it. There is no need for these facilities to be elaborate. Work areas can be as simple as a folding table and a beach umbrella, or as extravagant as a luxurious building with electronically controlled water, heat, light, and humidity. Between these extremes there are many alternatives, orthodox and unusual, some of which are suggested here.

Storage Areas

Having an airtight, possibly lockable storage facility on the roof will make many gardening jobs easier, keep rain and humidity away from your supplies, and help keep the garden neat and your equipment readily available. By having soil constituents, containers, and tools in one place, they are not only easy to find, but you can keep track of inventories. A shed can also help you shield your garden from pollution, wind, or noise and give you a surface for planting against or a support for a potting bench, awning, arbor, or trellis, depending on location and size.

If you can find a niche somewhere out of the rain, an old Army *footlocker or steamer trunk* can be adapted for storage, and most can be locked with a padlock. They are commonly for sale at flea markets and garage sales, where they should be inexpensive. Sears and many other lawn/hardware centers offer a *weather-proof storage locker* with secure, sliding doors on the top and side. With twenty to thirty square feet of space, the lockers could store two half-bushel bags of soil, peat, or vermiculite as well as tools, hoses, and containers, or a small group of dormant plants in containers for winter protection. The *steel closets*—which are manufactured in many shapes, with sliding or hinged doors and with or without shelves—sold in department and hardware stores are also useful. They may, however, rust if left in the rain, and they tend to get hot if they are in the sun. *Trash cans,* particularly thirty-gallon heavy-gauge plastic models, are good for storing soil, hoses, tools, and other supplies which you wish to keep dry and out of the way. They offer several advantages, being lightweight, easy to move and store, easy to wash and quiet to use. Trash cans have to be locked into a shed or rack of some type for security, however, since they cannot be padlocked. They are sold all over, in several sizes and shapes and in a wide range of prices.

If your need is primarily for security and not for appearance or weather protection, you can make or buy an enclosure of *chain-link fencing,* with or without a top and slats for opacity. Despite its relatively open construction, when properly anchored, this type of enclosure is probably most secure of all the sheds described here. A less secure, but probably more decorative, open shed of wood may also be helpful, either in conjunction with waterproof trash cans or alone. It is much less expensive to build, as you can use scrap lengths of 2 × 4s, 4 × 4s, or 2 × 6s, and it can be built to fit any odd corner of your roof. Wooden storage sheds can easily be the nucleus of a work/storage/shade unit, to be built at once or in modular stages when time and money permit.

Small *metal sheds,* complete with roofs, interior shelves, lockable doors, and coated siding, are sold at Sears, garden centers, and discount stores. Disguising or naturalizing these sheds can be a major problem. They are probably meant to be hidden somewhere behind a garage or a grove of trees—things in fairly short supply on the average

Useful Storage Facilities

Plastic trashcans are useful for storage, mixing soil, etc.

Metal storage locker with sliding doors at side and top has many uses. It will hold two trash cans, bags of soil, tools, etc. Available from Sears, Penney, garden centers, and hardware stores.

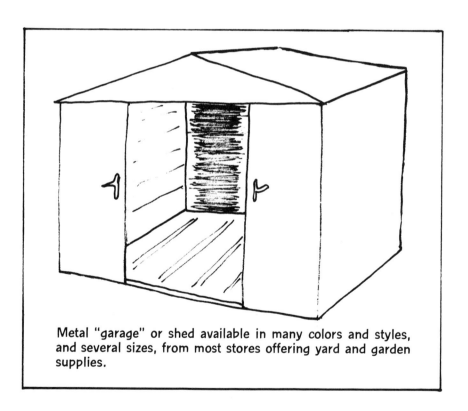

Metal "garage" or shed available in many colors and styles, and several sizes, from most stores offering yard and garden supplies.

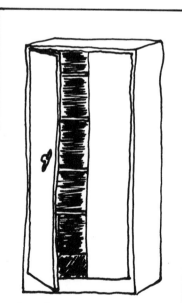

Steel storage cabinets manufactured for home and office use, with either hinged or sliding doors.

You can store soil, supplies, and tools in almost any waterproof container, but these are especially well suited to roof gardens.

city roof where one of these metal monsters will stand out as perhaps the ugliest structure around. However, a complete 10 × 10-foot shed with doors will cost about $150, and if you aren't particularly handy but need the storage space, this is a pretty good bargain. The sheds are usually made of corrugated metal, enameled in white (which will reflect heat but create glare) and some colors, usually including dark green and reddish brown. These metal sheds are lightweight, but on a tar paper roof you should make a foundation framework of wood to prevent damage to the roof and to secure the shed against being blown off in storms or heavy wind. You can attach a framework of 2 × 4s to the roof, then bolt the shed to the frame; cover the screws with roofing cement for watertightness. Most of the sheds have no floor of their own, so you can combine the wooden support with a decking floor, which will protect plants and stored materials from moisture damage and insects and prevent these things from damaging the roof surface. Some towns have ordinances concerning the placement of these sheds. While the laws are usually directed toward street-level gardens, they may be enforced everywhere. Your city's building department should be able to advise you.

Work Areas

A work area is useful, if only because it enables you to leave other tables and benches clean and free for eating, reading, or other uses. A well-designed work area, of course, can also help you garden, by providing ready access for frequently used tools, containers, soil and water, and a counter of convenient height. What you do will more than likely depend on cost, space, and the permanence of your garden. Alternatives range from collapsible tables to beautiful combination work/storage areas with a shaded seating area, lath house for delicate plants, and other features.

Such a permanent investment as building directly on the roof may be too risky and expensive for many roof gardeners, particularly those who rent. A *folding metal table,* available at variety,

camping equipment, and department stores, usually for much less than fifty dollars (although there is a wide range in quality), may be a good alternative solution. It folds for storage and usually has a convenient handle for carrying up and down stairs, and it should last for three or more years if you don't habitually leave it in the rain. These tables are not very strong, and should probably not be used continually to support heavy objects.

Making a bench of *sawhorses and plywood* is in some ways a better solution, as both the size and height can be tailored to your space limitations and your working needs. Although old-fashioned all-wood sawhorses can be built easily enough, you will achieve greater strength and rigidity by using metal sawhorse brackets, which come in two types. The one which uses bolts, not nails, to hold the 2 × 4s is more flexible, as it allows you to disassemble them for storage or to change the size or height for different purposes. The bolt-using brackets are sold at Sears and other sophisticated—not necessarily neighborhood—hardware stores. A 3 × 6-foot sheet of nominal 1-inch plywood (actually about ¾ inch thick), supported on two 2½-foot-wide sawhorses spaced 5 feet apart, at any height up to about 4 feet, will be sturdier than the folding table, and probably cheaper to assemble. Thinner plywood can be used for a shorter span, but as you increase the distance between the sawhorses, you weaken the support, thus requiring heavier plywood.

If space permits, you can construct a *bench of 2 × 4s and 4-inch planks.* If permanence would be a problem, the unit can be assembled with screws, rather than nails, for disassembly in the fall. You can also buy *steel workbench frames,* to which planks, pressed wood, or plywood can be bolted, although these are relatively expensive. They are strong, however, easy to take apart for storage, and flexible in use, as drawers, lower shelves, and tool racks can be fitted to them. Because the steel frame has bolt holes at regular intervals, it is easy to enclose the bench, attach a backboard or trellis, or make other adaptations without unusual tools or equipment. Uprights bolted to the bench frame can support an arbor or shade, serve to link modules—such as another bench, a sun deck, or heavy planters—to secure them to the roof. The

Old electric cable spools can make elegant tables for large roof gardens. This one has been built into a deck and surfaced in the same boards.

Most of these plants spend the rest of the year indoors. The delicate exotics spend the summer in the lath house, where they can thrive without exposure to full sun.

supports of wooden benches can function in the same ways, and may be less expensive to build, depending on lumber prices and whether or not you can find used or otherwise inexpensive steel framing. Constructing a bench entirely of wood, however, may require more tools than working with a steel frame, and it may violate fire regulations.

One of the difficulties of using a portable potting bench is that you (and the plants) are almost always exposed to the direct sun. If you build an arbor or a shaded area, even a small space which can be used for several purposes, you can, however, avoid such constant exposure. The area can be as small as 6 feet square and serve you well, although a larger area will require less rearrangement to permit both work and play. If you have access to a stairwell, elevator housing, water tower, or adjacent wall, one of the simplest and most substantial ways to build a shelter is to attach

it to one of these strong structures. If the structure is of brick, stone, or concrete, you can use a masonry bit in an electric drill to make holes, and expansion bolts (like the mollies used to mount indoor cabinets on the wall, only larger) to attach 2 × 4 wood braces. These can be used to support a workbench (with legs in front for extra strength and stability), an overhead frame for an arbor, or a rack for a canvas or plastic roof, or to build a storage shed.

There are good practical reasons for building a *freestanding work/storage/shelter area*, even though this may be a relatively expensive solution. For one, structures attached to any part of a building become fixed improvements and, legally if not practically, the property of the building owner. You may not be able to find a surface on which to attach the structures. Or you may wish to build

A close-up of the lath house—or gazebo, as its designer and owner, artist Lowell Nesbitt, prefers to call it. It not only shields fragile tropical plants from direct sun but provides a restful place to think as well.

Plywood makes strong worktables, though constant exposure to the weather may eventually cause its layers to buckle as shown in this picture.

something in the middle of your roof for aesthetic or gardening reasons. Whatever the reason, the sturdiest approach is to construct an open frame with a raised floor (probably duckboards). This structure can become the nucleus of an entire garden center, with storage, work space, compost and soil bins, a sink, an arbor and a seating area. The frame can be built of lumber, or of aluminum or steel pipe and special snap-on or screw-on connectors; in either case, many materials can be at-

tached to form walls or a roof. A classical arbor can be made by weaving laths, or you can buy plastic grids made to simulate woven lath at garden centers. You can achieve filtered light inexpensively and easily by stretching bamboo roll-up blinds across the upper frame. The blinds come in match-stick or half-bamboo patterns or in plastic made to look like bamboo, in a variety of colors and useful sizes. Unless you support them at several points, they will sag, however, and even the

The lath-strip screen echoes duckboard patterns as it shades a working/resting area.

plastic versions will only last a season or two before the threads which link them begin to disintegrate. Tubing—conduit or plastic plumbing pipe—can be stretched across the frame to help support the blinds, plants, fabric, or other coverings. If you build such a structure using screws rather than nails, which takes a little more work in the beginning, even such a complex, solidly built unit can be disassembled easily.

Less sturdy construction methods may do, of course, if your roof is sheltered from the wind, or if you need to cover a small area. If you have a deck, you can install tent poles at intervals and stretch a nylon or cotton canvas tarp across them, although this will not survive gusts of wind or storms, so it should probably be removed whenever you are not on the roof.

CONTAINERS

Possibly even more important than the roof and its fixtures are the containers you choose for your plants. A plant in a container needs all the help we can give it. No matter what it looks like—what color, shape, or material it is made of—the container must fit the plant. It must be large enough to hold the roots and sufficient soil to support the plant properly, to insulate against heat and cold, and to store and supply nutrients and water. In extremely hot or cold climates, the container itself should probably be an insulator; in strong or persistent winds, it should probably be nonporous.

Given an appropriate height to width relationship, almost any container can be used for plants so long as it has drainage holes in or near the bottom to permit excess water to escape. Not only do the holes allow water to drain, but the action of water passing through the soil is what draws nutrients and oxygen through the soil to support healthy root growth. While it is possible to grow plants, at least for a time, in containers without provision for drainage, it requires machine-like precision and a lot of luck. Eventually the plant is likely either to develop shallow roots, caused by anxious, frequent but shallow watering, or to die back from lack of oxygen at the roots, caused by overwatering. Really, no visual perfection (or laziness) is worth the difficulty of planting in a container without holes. By using an electric hand drill and a carbide-tipped drill bit, you can drill holes in virtually any material, including glass, ceramic, and stone. You can drill softer materials with a hand drill and regular bits.

While a container which breathes may allow the plant to dry out, it also encourages healthy growth by facilitating the passage of oxygen to the roots. On the other hand, nonporous containers, such as glazed or high-fired ceramic, plastic, metal, and heavily painted or varnished wood will retain moisture, an advantage in a windy garden.

You may choose either a porous or nonporous container for a plant, although each variety will theoretically do best in one or the other type. In practice, you can compensate for the loss of moisture through the walls of a porous container by mulching, double-containering, or insulating. A plant which needs a porous container can be grown in plastic or other nonporous material if you use a lighter than normal soil mixture and adjust your watering schedule. Most types of plants should have a container that is about as high or perhaps a little higher than its diameter (or diagonal). If it is too deep, you can use perlite or stones beneath the soil and plant, but if it is too shallow, you really cannot use it. All containers should be strong enough to hold the plant and moist soil without deforming or breaking. If a container is built too openly to hold soil, you can line the sides and bottom with sheet plastic such as inexpensive drop cloths or a cut-up trash bag, slashed at intervals for drainage, or with layers of newspaper or unmilled sphagnum moss. Any of these lining materials will hold soil and roots in until the plant is established and the roots grow to hold the soil. If you are concerned about a container's strength it can be reinforced with metal or plastic straps, strips of wood or waterproof polyester or nylon rope, wrapped around tautly several times. If you are conscientious, you should probably treat wooden containers to prevent moisture damage and rotting, but the process is time-consuming, smelly, and messy, particularly if you must do it indoors. It is sometimes worth gambling on the durability of the containers by leaving them untreated. I have seen wood crates, just as found in an industrial trash pile, last for two or three years without any preservative treatment. On the other hand, there is some risk—an untreated container may not last even a single summer. If you feel lazy about treating containers, a good compromise is to waterproof only those containers for valuable perennial specimen plants, leaving the ones used for annuals and vegetables alone.

Never before has there been such a range of materials and styles to choose from for plant containers. The blooming popularity of gardens of every size and style has apparently led manufacturers to supply containers to match. While you can generally select containers by appearance, cost, or availability, different materials offer different qualities, and these should also influence your choice. A plant which needs moist soil should be grown in a nonporous container, particularly on the roof, where steady sun and wind tend to dry the atmosphere and the plants. On a very hot roof, you may need to insulate your containers with half-inch sheets of expanded polystyrene (Styrofoam, for example) or use double containers or some other system to protect roots from accumulated heat. Matching your plant's needs to container materials will not only save work but may also make the difference between succeeding or failing with a borderline plant.

Terra cotta—Classical terra cotta (unglazed, low-fired red clay) tubs, which are more or less just large flowerpots, are still probably the most popular containers. They are practical and easy to find in sizes up to eighteen inches or so; larger sizes, though they exist, are sometimes harder to find. Terra cotta is a very useful material, as it breathes and facilitates the movement of water, nutrients, and oxygen to the plant roots. It looks at home in any garden and is relatively lightweight but strong. The shape of most terra cotta containers also makes repotting easy, as it flares out at the top. The porosity may be more of a problem than an advantage on a windy roof, however, as plants in clay containers need watering more frequently than those in nonporous containers, perhaps even twice as often in midsummer. Like wood, Styrofoam, and a few other plastics, terra cotta is a fairly good insulator, helping roots to stay cool in the sun despite the small amount of soil held by a container.

Terra cotta containers come in a wide range of styles and sizes, including some with molded patterns around the rim, the relatively rimless "Italian" pots, which are graceful but slightly weaker than the classical type with a reinforced band around the top, and special shapes, such as strawberry jars and hanging planters.

Other ceramics—Although they lack terra cotta's natural porosity, many other types of ceramic are used for planters. Aside from the imports available in the variety stores, most potters also have a line of hand-crafted containers, usually in both glazed and unglazed high-fired clays. Because the clay vitrifies in the high-temperature kiln, these are not quite the same as terra cotta, which they sometimes resemble. They are generally stronger,

The terra cotta pots on the pedestals are basic to gardens everywhere. The cast concrete planter in the center, however, needs a heavy-duty structure to support it.

less brittle, but nonporous, whether they are glazed or not. They can be made in almost any color, to harmonize with any setting, and they are highly recommended, assuming they have been made in appropriate depths and have good drainage holes.

Wood—Just as traditional and almost as popular as terra cotta, especially in larger sizes, are wooden tubs, usually square or octagonal and bound with metal bands. Like all containers, wooden tubs must have drainage holes in them even though wood is porous and there are usually cracks between the boards; as the wood absorbs moisture from the soil and expands, drainage from between the boards is obstructed. The wood may then begin to rot from the constant moisture.

The best wood for plant containers is probably redwood; it has natural resistance to the elements and withstands repeated soakings and dryings without splitting. Depending on your distance from California, however, the cost may be prohibitive. In other parts of the country you may find cedar or cypress more easily, and they are also suitable. You sometimes see tubs of other woods, like pine, anonymous construction lumber, plywood/or molded wood (which is not wood at all but a mixture of wood particles—that is, sawdust—and plastic). These share the virtues of all woods—they are good insulators, they are por-

A simple box of wood planks set on bricks works as well as any fancier planter, at least for a year or two.

ous (except for the plastic "wood") so they breathe slightly, and they look natural in the garden. But although you can use tubs of redwood, cedar, or cypress without preserving them, tubs of other woods (particularly pine and other softwoods) *should* be treated with Cuprinol or polyurethane varnish, especially if you are using them for valuable specimens. On the other hand, if you like to gamble, many untreated wooden containers have lasted year after year.

Plastics—Plastic is another popular material for containers. In fact, it is overtaking wood and clay in use, if not in esteem. Ubiquitous as plastic is, it is almost always introduced with an apology—it was all we could afford, it was the only material

Plastic containers of all types can be adapted for plants. Empty plastic flowerpots are shown at the left, and a washtub, a twenty-gallon trash can, and several wastebaskets hold large plants.

light enough to use on the roof, it was the only material of a pleasing color (or texture, or proportion, or something else) for the job. In fact, plastics (to lump together dozens of related materials) have begun to take over the container market. In gardening terms it makes sense: plastics have the ability to mimic almost any other material, including stone, clay, or wood, as well as stand proudly on their own distinctive merits. Plastic containers can be made to any gardening specification—for good insulation, massive or delicate appearance, high or low porosity—in any color, texture, pattern, or shape. They can be cast as wide shallow bowls too large to be formed economically in clay, or in interlocking modules which would be too heavy for the roof in concrete or traditional stone. Most plastics are nonreactive and nontoxic for plants, unlike some other materials, particularly concrete and some metals.

One of the most useful characteristics of plastic is its ability to insulate. While plants in the ground have literally tons of soil to help maintain an even root temperature, those in containers have very little; keeping roots cool is a special problem on the roof, with its lack of protection from sun. Because they can be molded in any color and texture, plastics can be made to reflect sunlight or, on the other hand, to absorb it to help prevent frozen soil and roots. Handsome plastic tubs are turning up more and more often at garden centers and plant departments, and if they continue to compete in price with traditional materials—a question today, as they are petroleum products—they will certainly replace them altogether.

Other materials—There are many other suitable materials for containers, although few of them are suitable for roof gardens. Changes in manufacturing and technology are driving some of these materials—too expensive, too heavy, or too out of style—from the marketplace. Carved and natural formations of *stone* were popular once, and still are for a few country estates, but today we are more likely to see plastic cast to look like stone than the real thing (or, perhaps as likely, expanded volcanic lava, marketed as Featherock). Not only are the old-time stone industries dying out, we generally have less space in modern gardens (and certainly on the roof) for the massive, decorated containers typical of stone. Containers of *metal*, particularly lead, were also popular once, but these have many drawbacks, particularly on the roof. Lead is definitely too heavy for most roofs—and probably for most people's wallets as well. Copper and brass, both expensive, may also react with nutrient solutions, producing an imbalance. Containers constructed of thin sheets of steel or aluminum are common, especially for window boxes but, without modification, they provide too little insulation against the sun to be really useful on the roof.

Found containers—Probably rivaling all commercially made planters in popularity are tubs and boxes diverted from industrial or food-handling purposes. These include nail kegs (if you can still find them), beer and wine barrels, Japanese soy tubs (now usually made of heavy gauge, flexible plastic instead of the old wood and bamboo), and all the other containers from the health food, produce, or grocery store, including bushel baskets, mushroom baskets, and heavy wooden crates of various shapes and sizes. These found containers vary in their strength and longevity, but weak ones can be banded, tied, or treated to endure at

Greek olives were originally packed in this tub, now used to raise a beefsteak tomato.

A sturdy wooden shipping crate.

least a season or two. Their initial cost (usually nothing) more than makes it worth your while to experiment. You might have to pay a dollar or so to induce someone to help you get some of the best of these containers, but they sometimes outlast specially made garden tubs, and they are often more lovely.

Chinese and Japanese food importers are an excellent source of interesting containers. The large green ceramic urns used to transport and sell preserved foods (like "hundred-year-old eggs") are sold (I found one for $30 in New York in 1975); they often have a crack in the bottom, but cracks can be patched with epoxy cement, and drainage holes can and should then be drilled in them. Other decorative and useful plant containers from the Oriental food stores are likely to be free. The strong reinforced crates used to ship all sorts of bottled and canned seasonings (like hoisin sauce and oyster sauce) and the narrow kegs used to carry and sell bean curd are free, and can be found discarded on the street in front of the stores in medium and large cities all over the country.

Vegetable stands throw out a variety of wonderful gardening containers. Mushroom baskets— deep oblongs (about 6 × 15 inches), complete with wire handle—now come with pierced plastic bottoms, which add strength. Baskets of berries

and other fruits come in shallow flats, and oranges, grapefruits, and apples come in strong wooden crates. Bushel baskets are still found in produce stores, and so are small berry boxes, now often molded of plastic. Any of these may require liners of plastic or sphagnum moss to keep the soil in, but are excellent in all other ways in the garden.

Pickle makers and meat processors use barrels—of traditional woods or, more likely nowadays, molded plastics—in every size from 5 to 100 gallons. These can be sawed to convenient height and drilled easily; they are especially good for shrubs or a group of vegetables. Milk crates of plastic or plastic-coated wire, lined for soil retention, make good portable containers, especially for vegetables and summer flowers.

Cheese importers throw away some wonderful containers, including lightweight shallow wooden trays, useful as flats for starting seeds in the spring, and larger, heavier crates, useful for annuals, vegetables, or small shrubs. Wine dealers have some wines delivered in wooden, rather than cardboard, boxes; these are shallow (8 to 10 inches) and about 18 inches square, strong and well made.

Industrial shipping crates—designed for heavy equipment or several cases of goods—are often excellent for planting in, as they are sturdy enough to hold moist soil. Plumbing suppliers also offer a few useful containers. Discarded bathtubs, washtubs, or other plumbing fixtures, filled with soil and abloom with flowers, are a familiar sight in the country, but many of these may be too heavy or cumbersome to take to the roof. Short lengths of ceramic or rigid plastic pipes (in large diameters), on the other hand, can be used in the roof garden, and discarded old-fashioned oak water closets with copper lining intact are wonderful for growing a few tomatoes or pole beans. Fifty-gallon steel drums make good planters, depending on what they used to hold. (Some petroleum compounds, herbicides and pesticides particularly, are toxic to plants and difficult to neutralize or remove.) You can usually have holes drilled or burned for drainage, and have the drum cut in half or cut to any useful height by a boilermaker or auto body shop for a small fee. Half

These pictures show my neighbor cutting oak barrels down for use in the garden. After cutting around a chalk line, he paints the exposed rim with asphaltum (roofing cement).

of such a drum is large enough for a willow tree or a small climbing vegetable garden.

From the hardware store, nail kegs are great containers for shrubs or vegetables, but they have become hard to find. Strong metal buckets, used for spackling compounds, roofing cement, and other construction materials, are homely but useful containers, especially for vegetables or other fast-growing annuals which can use depth. Chicken wire, plastic, bronze, aluminum or copper screening, or the metal mesh called hardware cloth, can be formed and wired together into cylinders for training tall or climbing vegetables or

filled with sphagnum moss for making freestanding columns for strawberries or flowering annuals.

From kitchen specialty stores, wire baskets designed for storing eggs or fruit come in many shapes and sizes; filled with sphagnum moss or soil, they make good hanging planters. Restaurant-weight stainless or aluminum baking pans, with holes added, make good planters for herbs or a few flowers. Sometimes used or second quality restaurant pans can be found—the sizes and weights are excellent for gardening, although they are never really cheap.

The variety store is a good source of inexpensive

Wine boxes are becoming scarce, but they are excellent for plants. This one rests on a skid.

A wooden packing crate from a machine tool manufacturer.

containers. Shoeboxes, hatboxes, cake or bread containers and other firm, transparent containers, particularly those with covers, are excellent for starting seeds and cuttings. Plastic wastepaper baskets, trash cans, plastic bowls, and refrigerator containers, all with holes cut or drilled in the bottom make useful containers for shrubs, flowers, or vegetables, and collanders, sieves, and laundry baskets, with ready-made holes, are also useful. All of these can be stacked easily and neatly away

for the winter. They come (sometimes unfortunately) in many colors, including a few which their makers seem to think resemble wood, ceramic, or copper, and in many shapes and sizes. The best thing about variety store plastic wares as plant containers is their availability—you can find something almost any day of the week, usually at modest cost.

Sometimes a local garage can be a surprising source of gardening containers. Old tires are use-

Visible here are wooden shipping crates, metal drums, plastic trash cans, and an oak barrel.

An old tire can be turned inside out and cut to make an amusing planter.

ful on the roof as a double container for tubs of plants which need additional insulation from the sun or cold, and they can be used—sometimes in odd ways—for growing in directly.

You can build containers—at least wooden ones—easily, using ordinary carpentry tools, or you can sometimes find a local fabricator who will do the job reasonably. This is certainly a more expensive procedure than finding usable shipping crates in the trash, but it is sometimes the only way to solve such problems as an oddly shaped corner, lack of space or the need to have a group of identical containers. Whether you plan to build yourself or have someone else do it, make detailed drawings (even crude ones) with all dimensions marked and double-checked before you proceed. For a wooden planter 30 inches long or less, nominal 1-inch boards are heavy enough; depending on depth, you can also get away with 1-inch boards for a longer container if you use reinforcement in the corners and along the bottom. In most cases, the simplest method of construction is probably best, especially if you have only a hand or saber saw and simple drill. Unless you intend to dismantle the containers for some reason, the best way to build them is with glued joints, reinforced with small nonrusting aluminum nails.

Keep in mind the basic needs of the plant: to have ample room for roots, to have drainage holes in the bottom and spacer bars beneath the container to permit air circulation and drainage, and to have protection from sun and wind. If you lack tools, you can ask to have wood cut to length at the lumberyard. Although they charge for this service, it may save you a lot of time and work, and their saws leave a smoother edge than hand tools do. You will then need only to drill holes and nail and glue the pieces together. Treating redwood, cypress, or cedar for water resistance is not necessary. Whether you need to preserve other types of wood or not depends on a number of factors discussed earlier, but preserving is recommended for longevity and strength.

3

Botany for a Roof Garden

Botany is the study of plants which, metaphorically speaking, are half of life on earth. Actually, depending on the system of measurement, plants outnumber animals considerably, but the two life forms are completely balanced. Plants are our kin—that is, we (the animals) and they are formed of similar basic cells and are bound inextricably in a cycle of mutual dependence. Plants give us pleasure, as well as the means to live, and their varieties are many and complex. As you increase your understanding of plants—the ways they grow and reproduce—you will also learn to enjoy and use them more extensively.

CLASSIFICATION OF GARDEN PLANTS

The plants people cultivate are separated into three classes based on the structure of their seeds, leaves, and stems: *filicineae, gymnosperms,* and *angiosperms. Filicineae,* the ferns, actually have no flowers or seeds, and reproduce by spores borne on the backs of generally compound lacy leaves, which have long-lived, tightly coiled growing tips. The leaves may be evergreen or deciduous, although most of the ferns grown in the North are deciduous. Most cone-bearing *gymnosperms* have woody stems, bear needle or scale-shaped leaves, and are evergreen. Flower-producing *angiosperms* have many different shapes, sizes, growth habits, and types of foliage, flowers, and fruit. They may be evergreen or deciduous and have either woody or herbaceous stems.

The angiosperms are further divided into two subclasses, *monocotyledons* and *dicotyledons,* based on whether their seeds contain one (*mono*) or two (*di*) seedleaves (*cotyledons*). In general, the monocots are simpler than the dicots. The two subclasses are often described as being either grass-like or oak-like, although dicots are not always trees. All of these classes and subclasses of plants have basic growth systems of roots, stems and leaves which work together to convert sunlight, water, and minerals (taken from the air and soil) to food.

THE STRUCTURE OF PLANTS

Roots

Roots are a plant's foundation. They absorb minerals, water, and oxygen from the soil, and transport these essentials, as well as previously manufactured and stored food, through the stems to the leaves. The roots anchor the plant to the soil, so wind and other influences cannot easily uproot it. All roots store at least small amounts of food at times, and some accumulate and store larger amounts on a nearly permanent basis. In most plants, there are more roots than top growth, although this cannot necessarily be measured by weight, volume, or length.

Roots are basically of two types. Some plants have a central, thrusting root—a *taproot*—from which smaller, secondary roots branch off. Some

Roots

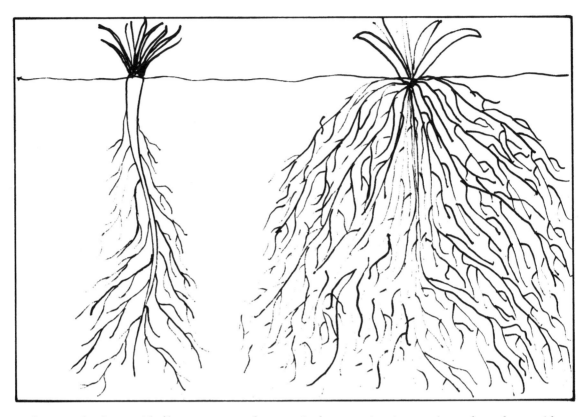

In general, plants with fibrous roots are better suited to growing in containers than plants with taproots. Some trees and shrubs which normally have taproot systems produce fibrous roots after being transplanted at the nursery, however; such plants are also good candidates for success on the roof. A typical taproot is shown at left and typical fibrous roots at right.

taproots, like those of carrots and radishes, are wide and fleshy at the top, and store large amounts of food. Others are narrow, but still clearly dominant. Some plants and the ferns, which have an underground rhizome, have *fibrous roots*—several sets of roots, no one central or clearly dominant, from which smaller and smaller tiers of roots branch off. In general fibrous-rooted plants grow better in containers than taprooted plants because the latter may suffer from lack of soil depth.

Roots function by absorbing water and nutrients from solutions held in the soil. Most of this absorption is achieved by the root hairs, tiny short-lived "hairs" which develop just behind a root's growing tip, so they are constantly in contact with new soil particles as the root lengthens

and moves through the soil. Usually, root hairs live for only a short time, so most absorption of growth essentials occurs through new growth, while older root structures transport the materials to the stems and store already manufactured food.

Stems and Buds

Stems transport nutrients, water, and previously manufactured food from the roots through the stems to the leaves, where they are used in photosynthesis, and transport food from the leaves to the roots for storage. Sometimes stems also store water and converted food. In addition to transporting and storing growth essentials, stems bear the buds which become leaves, flowers, and

Stems

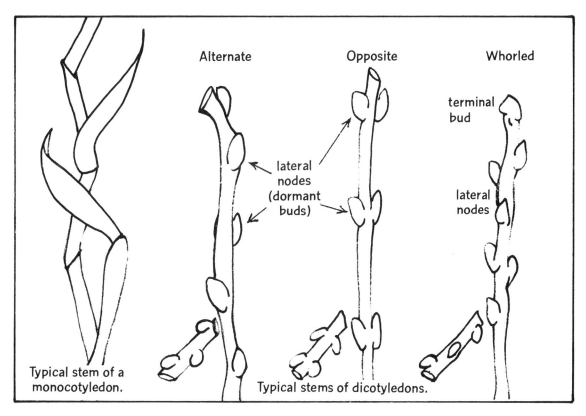

Understanding stem structure helps in identifying and pruning plants.

fruit, and support these organs in proper position for photosynthesis, pollination, or other processes to occur. Tree trunks are stems, as are stalks of grass, weeping willow branches, and rhizomes of ferns, and strawberry runners.

In dicots, buds usually form in the *leaf axil*, which is the joint of a leaf stalk and the stem. A widened, calloused ring, called a *node*, forms at the point where the leaf and bud attach to the stem; the spaces between these nodes are called *internodes*. Although plants have their own distinctive growth patterns, environmental conditions—lack of light or uneven light, particularly—may alter the length of the internodes in any particular specimen.

You can describe buds in various ways, one of which is by function. Each bud will produce leaves, flowers, or a mixture—usually a flower with altered leaves, or bracts, at the base or around it. Buds can also be described by their placement on the stem: *terminal buds* are the growing tips of stems; *lateral* (or *axillary*) *buds* grow in leaf axils along the stem; *accessory buds* cluster around another, dominant (usually leaf) buds; and *adventitious buds* appear almost anywhere on a stem, usually after pruning or accidental damage to the primary buds. Terminal buds are usually the most vigorous; they may be active while lateral buds on the same stem are dormant. If you pinch out the terminal bud, however, lateral buds may then develop, which is one way to induce branching and bushiness in some plants.

Most other bud characteristics are more helpful in distinguishing one plant from another than for improving their culture. Unfortunately, it is often difficult to tell by looking at dormant buds whether they will produce leaves or flowers, though sometimes leaf and flower buds differ in appearance—flower buds are fuller and may reveal a hint of petal color—and sometimes in placement—a central bud in a group is likely to be a leaf bud, which is dominant, with accessory flower buds around it. Ordinarily, there are more leaf buds than flower buds on a plant. Buds form in the spring on most plants, but on others— rhododendrons, for example—they form in the fall and live through the winter. It is important to know the budding patterns of the plants in your garden so you can avoid pruning off next year's growth and provide appropriate winter protection when needed.

Certain plants, the monocots, have a single stem with a single growing tip. If you remove it, the plant may die. Such plants include most of the grains—corn, wheat, the grasses—and some tropical trees, such as the palms. Generally, monocots are easy to recognize, even when young, as they look somewhat like grass, with a growing tip and no regular nodes or lateral buds.

In ferns, conifers, and most dicots, both woody and herbaceous, stems are complex, having several groups of cells with clearly defined functions. The *epidermis*, somewhat analogous to human skin, is a shallow layer protecting the functioning stem from the environment. It retains normal moisture and rejects external liquids, dusts, and vapors, thus protecting the tissue within from contamination. It also protects against superficial wounds. The next group of layers is the *cortex*. Specialized cortical tissues store water and food, aid in photosynthesis, control plant secretions, give strength and elasticity to the stem, and distribute chloroplasts which make the foliage green. The cortex essentially controls mechanical functions.

Finally, there are the *vascular tissues or bundles,* which transport water, nutrients, food, and other substances within the plant. Each of these bundles surrounds a large-celled food storage chamber, called the *pith*. The rhizome of a fern is a complex stem but it differs from the stems of dicots primarily in its organization, while the layers in monocots are often less specialized, scattered rather than arranged in rings, and functionally simpler.

Bulbs, corms, rhizomes, runners or *stolons, tendrils* and *tubers* are all specialized forms of stems, even though some of them appear to be roots. The dis-

tinction is practical as well as technical—roots lack nodes or buds, which are necessary for propagation.

Leaves

By *photosynthesis,* plants use sunlight to manufacture food—organic compounds like starches, sugars, fats, and proteins—from minerals absorbed from the air and soil. Photosynthesis can only occur in cells containing chlorophyll, and most of these cells are in the leaves (the stems also may have a few). By *transpiration,* leaves give off water absorbed by the roots. Since photosynthesis is an energy-converting process, it gives off waste products—oxygen and water, for example—and consumes raw materials—carbon dioxide, mineral salts taken from solutions in the soil, for example. The movement of these materials through the plant is by diffusion, controlled by differences in "pressure" from soil and air to plant, from cell to cell within the plant, and from plant to air at the leaves. If pressures are equalized or reversed at any point, the process stops.

Leaves are usually thin and flat, maximizing surface area and facilitating both photosynthesis and transpiration. The gymnosperms have *needle or scale-shaped* leaves; angiosperms have leaves of many different shapes, but these may be classified as either *simple* (solid) or *compound* (segmented). Ferns usually have compound leaves, some of them in lacy patterns. Monocot leaves tend to have parallel veins, while dicots have netted veins; monocots have a sheath from which the leaf—flat, tubular, or fan-shaped—emerges; dicots almost always have a *petiole* (stalk) of varying length with the leaf attached to it. The petiole and, to a lesser degree, the leaf are extensions of the stem. The epidermis continues into these organs, in somewhat altered form, covers the top and bottom of the leaf. The vascular bundles become the leaf veins. Beneath the epidermis is the *mesophyll,* which is the site of photosynthesis. The epidermis has openings (*stomata*) through which gases pass in both directions—carbon dioxide in and oxygen out. The stomata are surrounded by guard cells, which respond to changes in light, temperature, and humidity by opening or closing the stomata.

Deciduous Leaf Shapes

Simple (solid) leaves

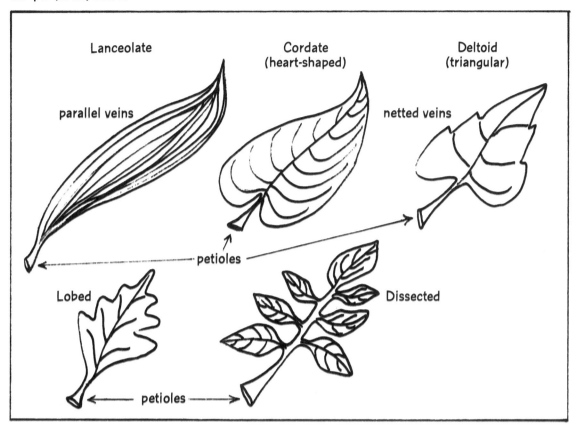

Compound (segmented) leaves

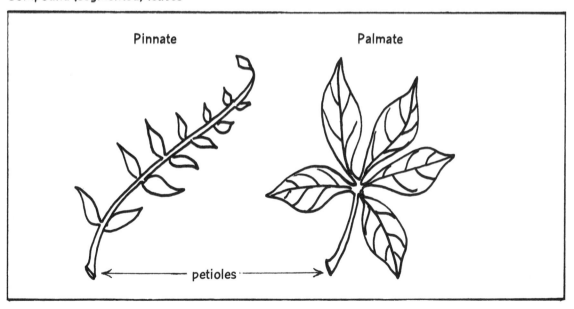

A knowledge of basic leaf shapes is essential for identifying mature plants.

The *spines* of cactus, *tendrils* of peas, *bracts* of poinsettias and the flower-like *insect-eating parts* of such plants as Venus flytrap are all specialized leaf forms.

Reproductive Structures of Seed-bearing Plants

All seed-bearing plants—that is, all the garden plants except true mosses, ferns, and mushrooms—produce flowers and fruit during their life cycle. The flower is the plant's reproductive system, and the fruit is the seed covering; either of these organs can be single or multiple, obvious or hard to find, and either can take a variety of forms.

Flowers—Complete flowers have four organs, usually concentrically arranged around the *receptacle* (the place where the flower joins the stem). These organs are listed here, in order from the outside.

1. The *calyx,* formed of *sepals,* which are specialized leaves, usually green but sometimes colored, which shield the blossom before it opens and then remain at its base.

2. The *corolla,* formed of *petals,* the soft, usually gaily colored parts which are valued for their color, scent, and texture.

3. The *androecium* or male organ, formed of *stamens,* a slender, upright stalk (the *filament*) with the pollen-producing *anther* at the tip.

4. The *genoecium,* or female organ, formed of *carpels,* which include one or more *pistils,* jug-shaped organs formed of an *ovary* (containing eggs or *ovules*) on the bottom, an elongated neck (*style*) and a mouth (*stigma*).

Incomplete flowers lack one or more of the four organs. Some flowers lack sepals or petals or both, or have these organs in such unusual shapes, positions, colors, or textures that they are hard to identify. *Perfect* (or *hermaphroditic*) flowers bear both male and female parts; *imperfect* (*unisexual*) flowers—that is flowers with only *pistillate* (female) or *staminate* (male) parts—may be either *monoecious* (with both male and female flowers on a plant) or *dioecious* (with only male or female flowers on each plant).

Flowers may be *regular* (or symmetrical) in structure with petals of equal size and shape radiating evenly from the center, like daisies, roses, and day lilies, or *irregular,* in a variety of patterns, like sweet peas, irises, or pansies. Flowers may occur singly, like all of the examples mentioned above, or in groups, like snapdragons, allium, or lupines, and they may be erect on their stems or drooping. Most of the differences in flower structures are more helpful for identifying a plant than for taking care of it. In some cases you may have to hand-pollinate, however, which will require you to identify the appropriate organs and determine when they are ready for pollinization.

Fruit—Technically, fruit is a mature ovary. The term includes not only such fruits as apples, apricots, and cherries, which we can readily identify, but pine cones, vegetables, nuts, and cereals as well. The form of the fruit is related to the structure of its flower. Basically, fruits may be classified as *simple* (formed from a single ovary), examples of which are peas, cherries, and walnuts; *aggregate* (formed from several ovaries in a single flower), such as blackberries and strawberries (these may also be described as clusters of simple fruits); and *multiple* (formed from ovaries of several flowers), as the pineapple. What we eat as the "fruit" or "seed" of a plant may include the entire mature ovary, seed, coating, and shell as in the tomato or only a part of it such as the flesh of peaches. Again, these distinctions are more useful to help sort out and identify plants than to care for them, but there are occasions, especially when reading gardening encyclopedias, when the information is useful.

As far as nature is concerned, fruits are designed to protect the seed and to assist its dissemination at the right time and place, thus to ensure the continuation of the species. To accomplish this, fruits have various forms and structures. Some are winged, to permit passage by air, some are waterproof and light so they can float in water, while others are burred so animals can carry them away attached to their fur or clothing. The seeds of most of our garden plants are disseminated—and germinated, fertilized, and consumed—by us.

Seeds also come in a wide variety of shapes and sizes, as distinctive as fingerprints in human beings, but all possess an *embryo* (the fertilized

Parts of the Flower

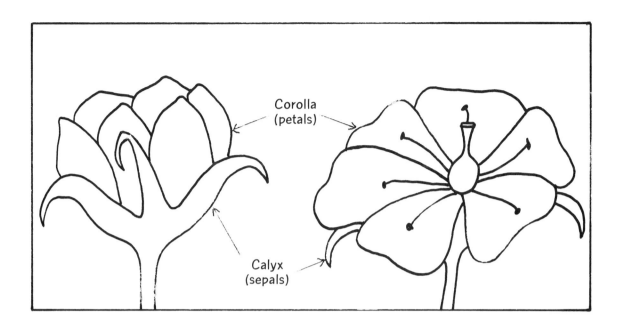

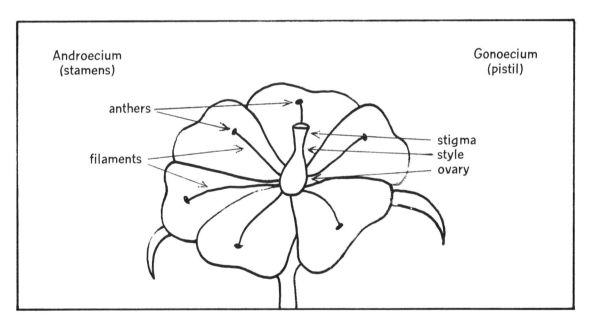

These drawings show the reproductive organs of a complete, regular flower.

ovule), which contains what botany students jocularly refer to as the shoot (*cotyledons* or seedleaves and *epicotyl* and *hypocotyl* or growing tip, stem, and true leaves) and the root (*radicle* or embryonic root). Seeds also contain a food supply (usually in tissue called the *endosperm*) and they are covered by a *seed coat*. While the seed's food supply is primarily intended to support the plant until its organs are mature enough to draw energy from the sun and the soil, the seed is also often the major storage area for food produced through photosynthesis, and our reason for growing the plant.

Reproductive Structures of
Non–Seed-bearing Plants

Spores—Ferns go through a two-phase reproductive process which distinguishes them from
conifers or flowering plants and which involves
somewhat different organs. *Spores* grow in *sporan-*
gia (spore cases) in a variety of patterns on the
undersides of fern leaves. When ripe, a small
whip-like organ (the *annulus*) thrusts the spores
onto the ground where they, through cell-
division, form small *gametophytes* or *prothallia*
(heart-shaped plantlets). Each of these possesses
microscopic male and female organs (*antheridia*
and *archegonia* respectively), which merge when
ripe, fertilizing one ovum per plant (though each
tiny plant may have more than one). The fertilized
egg produces a root and a shoot with the first fern
leaf, and the plant begins its cycle as a *sporophyte*
(spore-producer).

Mushroom reproduction also employs a form of
spores, but their culture is so difficult that few
attempt it, and it is not well suited to roof gardens.

HOW PLANTS GROW, BEAR
FRUIT, AND REPRODUCE

Plants are not self-sufficient organisms, capable
of creating food out of nothing. In order to live,
reproduce, and manufacture food, plants need
light, water, air, mineral nutrients, and a supportive environment.

Growth Processes

Light—The sun is ultimately the source of all the
energy on earth. *Photosynthesis* is the process by
which special green cells (*chloroplasts*) convert
nonstorable solar energy, carbon dioxide, and
water to storable chemical energy, or food. *Tran-*
spiration uses solar energy in the form of heat to
regulate plant growth, including photosynthesis,
by controlling the movement of moisture through
the plant and its subsequent release to the atmosphere. These and other growth processes use light
as their energy source.

Photosynthesis—Reduced to its barest essentials,
photosynthesis is the process by which plants
change carbon dioxide and water into sugar and
oxygen. The conversion requires light energy and
chloroplasts; the oxygen produced is released to
the air and the sugar is changed into other
carbohydrates for storage and later use by the
plant (or by animals which eat plants). The rate of
photosynthesis fluctuates in response to both
internal and external factors which affect the
availability of materials essential to the process.
The leaves of some plants have fewer chloroplasts
than others, thus slowing photosynthesis directly;
leaves of others have fewer or smaller stomata,
thus slowing the process indirectly, by restricting
the intake of carbon dioxide and the rate of transpiration. If there is insufficient water—caused by
low soil reserves, root damage, or too rapid
transpiration—the rate of photosynthesis will also
slow or stop. Different plants have different temperature ranges, light conditions, and carbon
dioxide concentrations which influence photosynthesis; too much of any of these critical factors may
retard the process, as may too little. Usually, the
optimum conditions for any plant are those normal to its natural environment.

A lack of carbon dioxide is likely to restrict or
prevent photosynthesis. This gas is continuously
collected from the air by leaf stomata, and dissolved in water stored in the leaf until it is called
on for use in photosynthesis, which is completely
dependent on the supply of carbon dioxide. Its
source is air, but air normally contains only a tiny
amount (.03 percent) of carbon dioxide, much less
than the earth's plants require. In order that
photosynthesis may occur, then, carbon dioxide
must be generated and released to the air continuously to replace that consumed by plants. The gas
is given off in respiration by plants and animals;
dead animals and plants and animal waste
products also release carbon dioxide in decomposition, and it is released in burning. But rarely
even all of these sources are inadequate, an occurrence which is much more likely in a
greenhouse than on an open roof. Under those
circumstances photosynthesis will slow or stop,
even if light and water are available in adequate
amounts.

Transpiration—Growing plants are primarily water—water permeates cell tissues and spaces between the cells are saturated with vapor. As long as the air around the plant contains less moisture than the plant cells, which is the case most of the time, and there is a source of light, the plant gives off water as vapor by diffusion from the leaf stomata. As this happens the leaf cells take moisture from adjacent cells and surrounding spaces, and so on throughout the plant, ultimately resulting in additional absorption by the roots. The process by which a plant loses or evaporates water to the air as vapor is transpiration, and it is fueled by heat energy absorbed by the plant as light. Transpiration is necessary for growth. It is also one of the principal ways water held by the soil is returned to the atmosphere. A fast-growing plant, like many vegetables, may transpire two quarts of water a day.

Many internal and external factors affect the rate of transpiration. For one thing, plants vary in their normal rate. Some of them have mechanisms for conserving moisture, such as recessed stomata or reduced numbers or sizes of stomata, possibly because their natural habitat is windy or arid, or because they are particularly susceptible to wilting. Others have "improved" root systems which permit faster or more efficient absorption or storage of soil water. Some plants have "panic" responses, such as the ability to close or fold up leaves, which temporarily reduce or halt transpiration. Transpiration will also diminish if either the intake of water by the roots or the release of vapor by the leaf stomata is interrupted. Cold air around the leaves or cold soil around the roots will thus slow transpiration.

Moisture can leave a plant only to the extent that the surrounding air can absorb it, so relative atmospheric humidity—throughout a region or just in your garden—also affects the transpiration rate. A brisk wind is likely to keep local humidity low by continuously bringing in drier air. Light wind or no wind, on the other hand, may permit a humid zone to develop around plants regardless of regional climate, because moisture previously transpired may remain a little longer in the air. In general, the faster air moves around a plant, the faster the rate of transpiration. However, transpiration will stop if for any reason the roots cannot absorb sufficient water. If the transpiration rate is high, on a hot, dry, windy day for example, the roots may not be able to keep up. If this happens, or if the roots are damaged or the soil is allowed to dry out, the leaf stomata will close and transpiration will cease. High air temperatures influence the rate of transpiration, in at least two ways: for one, warm air can hold more moisture than cold air, so an increase in air temperature brings about a lower relative humidity rating automatically. For another, higher temperatures increase the activity of most chemical processes, including transpiration.

Similarly, increases in light intensity stimulate the stomata of some plants to open, raise temperatures, and increase the rate of transpiration. Soil conditions which may slow or stop transpiration include not only lack of moisture and cold, but too much moisture (no air spaces) or too high a concentration of nutrients in solution in the soil caused by overfertilizing, low soil acidity, or failure to allow containers to drain from the bottom.

Respiration—Photosynthesis and transpiration use solar energy directly; other growth processes use it indirectly, through respiration, the complex process by which plants convert mineral nutrients and oxygen in reactions which release carbon dioxide to the atmosphere. If transpiration is the system of controlling fluids in a plant, respiration is the system of controlling gases. If respiration is blocked, so will be photosynthesis, transpiration, and growth in general.

Other growth processes using light—Light affects plants directly and indirectly in many essential growth processes other than photosynthesis and transpiration. Some of the responses are interrelated, like the production of chlorophyll, which gives plants their green color and is necessary to photosynthesis. Plant organs respond to light intensity, or the amount of energy received; to light quality, or the specific rays or wave-lengths received; and to light duration, the length of time light is received. The effects of light are also interrelated with those of temperature, weather, water, air, and soil.

Ordinarily, plants will not grow in the dark, but most will grow in less than optimum light conditions (short of absolute darkness) for at least brief periods. The growth produced, however, will be pale in color, leaves will be small, and stems will be elongated between the nodes. Plants grown only in red light may behave like plants grown in the dark, and many plants will fail to flower or to make seeds in light of lower intensity, greater or less duration, or wave-lengths other than they need, even though they may be able to grow to maturity under those conditions. Plants respond to light on a cellular level by growing toward it (*phototropism*); this is a response to a light coming from another direction than directly overhead, and it is a mechanism by which a plant attempts to compensate for a lack of good overhead light.

Water—Without water, plants die. Mineral nutrients can be absorbed and used only when dissolved in water, and it is also the source of oxygen and hydrogen required for photosynthesis, transpiration, and other growth processes. Plants are 90 percent water; it keeps plant cells and intercellular spaces saturated so nutrients can be moved into and through the plant by diffusion. Water enables roots to penetrate the soil by loosening the particles, and it permits air to follow through the soil in passages it has created. Decomposition of organic material requires water, and conversion of mineral nutrients to soluble ions accessible to plants often depends on gases dissolved in water.

Carbon dioxide is a minor component of air. It contains atoms of carbon and oxygen, which are necessary for a plant to make food. Plants consume carbon dioxide in photosynthesis and give it off in respiration, and it is the plant's only source of carbon.

Oxygen is a major component of air and water, and it is essential to photosynthesis and respiration. Although oxygen is plentiful in the environment, compacted soils prevent it from being available to the roots, which must have oxygen to function.

Mineral nutrients (or salts or ions) are the elements used in and essential to plant growth processes, and they are derived from the rock fragments which are the basis of soil. They are ions, dissolved in water held in the soil, from which solution they can be absorbed by plant roots. These elements, plus carbon, hydrogen, and oxy-

gen taken from air and water around the plant, are the essential elements of growth, but no soil naturally contains all of them in the proper proportion, and the use of sterile soil or soil-less mediums may require that you supply them in the form of organic supplements, chemical fertilizer, or a combination.

The "Big Three," or the macronutrients—nitrogen, phosphorus, and potassium—are the major elements required by volume. Fertilizers, which are mineral nutrients in their elemental (pure) form, are described by their proportions of these three nutrients, and some of them have little else. The fertilizer ratings always use the same order— that is, 6-12-6 always means 6 percent nitrogen (N), 12 percent phosphorus (P), 6 percent potassium (K). This ratio is sometimes called the N-P-K ratio. Other elements may or may not be present as well; to find that out, and the forms of all the included elements, read the labels.

Nitrogen is necessary for the formation of protein, and it controls growth. A deficiency is signaled by yellowing of leaves and stunting of growth. An excess prevents fruit and flower development. Although it is plentiful in the atmosphere, plants cannot take nitrogen directly from the air. It must be made available in the form of nitrates, ammonia or ammonia compounds, and amides, such as urea, present in the soil. There are also bacteria which capture nitrogen from air while living on the roots of certain plants such as peas and beans, and then release usable nitrogen to adjacent plant roots as needed. Nitrogen is easily leached out of the soil by water, and it should be supplemented regularly, particularly during active growth (the entire season for vegetables and flowering annuals), and particularly in well-drained soils (as yours should be). Good sources include chemical fertilizers, fish emulsion, bone meal (which is actually principally a source of phosphorus), and activated sewage sludge.

Phosphorus is necessary for the transfer of energy within the plant; it controls root growth and young, rapidly growing parts of the plant. A deficiency resembles nitrogen deficiency, except the foliage may develop amethyst tints, and root growth may be noticeably retarded. An excess of phosphorus is rare, since the element tends to form compounds (especially in acid soils) from which it does not go readily into solution. Phosphorus can be supplemented with bone meal and superphosphates (applied with care), as well as in chemical form.

Potassium provides the "mortar" (or "glue") between plant cells. It controls cell division and migrates from older to rapidly growing parts in case of a deficiency. Consequently, a lack of potassium slows growth generally, and older leaves, from which the mineral is withdrawn in favor of new growth, look scorched or bleached, especially on the tips and around the edges. It is difficult to have an excess of potassium, as only 1 percent of that present in the soil is available to plants. Good sources include chemical fertilizers and fresh hardwood ashes.

Secondary nutrients are not secondary in importance, but in volume. They are not less necessary to the plants, but they are required in smaller quantities than the macronutrients.

Sulfur (S) controls foliage and root development. A deficiency, a rare occurrence, may cause pale foliage to develop.

Calcium (Ca) controls cell growth and root development. Deficiencies are rare, but excesses are toxic.

Magnesium (Ma) is a component of chlorophyll. A deficiency causes chlorotic (bleached) leaves.

Trace elements or micronutrients are needed in tiny amounts, although they are not less necessary than the other minerals. Their specific roles in plant metabolism, however, are not always fully understood.

Iron (Fe) is required for the formation of chlorophyll. A deficiency causes chlorosis (leaf bleaching), but deficiencies in the mineral itself are actually rare. The mineral is sometimes unavailable to plants, however, due to a lack of soil acidity. Symptoms of a deficiency are often treated by changing the chemical balance of the soil.

Boron (B) is a growth regulator. A deficiency causes freaks, but it is rare. An excess, on the other hand, can kill—in fact, it is actually used as an herbicide in the borate form.

Zinc (Zn) is a growth regulator. A deficiency causes leaf abnormalities; an excess is toxic.

Manganese (Mn)—A deficiency may cause bleaching of the entire leaf, veins included.

Copper (Cu) is a growth regulator. A deficiency seems to cause freaks, particularly of plants grown in marshy or peaty soils.

Molybdenum (Mo) is necessary for normal growth and nitrate usage. An excess is toxic.

Chlorine (Cl) is necessary in minute quantities, and an excess is toxic to some susceptible plants. The amount present in chlorinated city water, however, is not normally a problem with the majority of plants.

Reproduction Processes

Plants may be reproduced *sexually* (by seed) or *asexually* or *vegetatively* (by cuttings, layering, etc.). Most gardeners use all of these means, at different times or for different types of plants, and you will need to understand all of them.

Sexual reproduction—Reproduction by seed is a sexual process because it begins with the union of male and female cells, and proceeds by division. The process essentially consists of three phases: *pollinization, fertilization,* and *germination.* Pollinization is the process by which mature pollen is transferred from an anther, where it is produced, to a pistil, where it can fertilize an ovule. Pollen and ovule may come from the same flower, from two flowers on a single plant, or from flowers on separate plants. Whatever the physical source, it is considered *self-pollinization* if the anther and stigma have identical genes and *cross-pollinization* if there are any genetic differences. The pollen may be transported in many ways. Wind and insects (usually bees) are the most common pollinating agents; plants which rely on wind usually produce huge amounts of winged or feathery pollen to ensure distribution. Pollen from flowering plants is generally less voluminous, and sticky to assist its adhesion to insect body parts. Some plants must be cross-pollinated. This group includes blueberries, many types of orchard trees which are self-sterile and grafted from the same rootstock so they are genetically identical, and certain marginal plants which will produce fruit by their own pollen but which produce better when pollinated by another genetic line. Certain familiar garden plants need assistance in pollination or hand-pollination, particularly in a small or isolated garden which is sheltered from the wind or attracts too few insects to ensure pollination. Generally, seed packets, labels on plants at the nursery, or plant descriptions in books warn you if the plant requires hand- or cross-pollination; these are not necessarily to be avoided because the pollinating procedures are simple.

If conditions are appropriate after pollinization, the grain of pollen bursts on the stigma and thrusts a stalk-like organ down into the ovary, and an ovule is fertilized. This process generates a single seed. Many grains of pollen fail to fertilize an ovule, and many seeds are consumed or fail to germinate. Fertilization triggers a number of changes in the flower; usually, petals drop and the reproductive organs wither away while the embryo plant develops in the ovary. This process is very clear in the pea, where the increasingly transparent petals of the flower surround the growing pod.

Actually, two cells from each grain of pollen fertilize each ovule, one forming the embryo or seed, the other forming the endosperm or food supply. If conditions are appropriate, the seed grows to maturity, undergoes a process of dormancy, and is ultimately germinated. There are many variations of this cycle, however. The food supply may be consumed by the growing seed as it develops (as in beans), or a food supply may enlarge (as in beets). The dormancy period may be measured in days, months, or even years, and it may be affected by time alone, or by patterns of temperature and moisture variation as well. Germination occurs when vital seed is placed in contact with an appropriately moist and warm growing medium. First the root emerges from the seed and grows downward in search of moisture and nourishment. Shortly thereafter, the seedling pushes up through the medium to light. Between the emergence of the root and the seedling, the embryo is dependent on the seed's food supply; if the soil lies too deeply over the seed, or if it is crusted, the seedling may die before it reaches light. It is basically for this reason that seeds are planted no deeper than their thickness. Most dicots push their seed leaves (cotyledons) up first, later producing true leaves which typify mature foliage. The grasses (monocots) and a few dicots (notably peas) retain seed leaves below the soil, so the first leaves to appear are the true leaves. In either case, once the foliage leaves emerge, the roots and foliage can be assumed to be functioning, and the plant ready for transplanting.

4

A Supportive Environment

A plant has a complicated relationship with the soil and atmosphere which support it. In any garden that environment includes not only natural but other conditions, altered or altogether provided by the gardener. On a roof you must supply more of the essential elements of a plant's environment than even the most technological farmer, because roofs offer so few plant necessities in a relatively natural form. In order to tamper with nature this way, the wise roof gardener acquires a working knowledge of how a plant depends on its environment, particularly soil and the atmosphere.

SOIL (OR A SOIL SUBSTITUTE)

All gardening begins with soils, those useful mixtures which hold a balance of air and water and nutrients and water so they are available to a plant's roots, support a plant so it can grow and draw energy from the sun, and insulate it from extremes of heat and cold. Of the essentials for plant growth—light, water, air, and mineral nutrients—all but light come at least in part through the soil. Although more or less natural soils have been the basis of gardening, soil-less mixtures, humus, or nutrient solutions alone can be formulated to support plants.

No matter where you find the soil you use, whether it is dug from a garden somewhere or bought as bags of inert ingredients from a nur-

sery, it will need modification to satisfy roof gardening conditions and even the needs of specific plants. Whether you use the synthetic mixture I recommend or real soil, the mixture you choose and how you use it will determine the success of your garden, so it is important to understand what soils do and how they do it. The term *soil*, incidentally, is used in this book to mean any material in which plants grow, unless a distinction is being made between synthetic and natural soils.

Composition of natural soils—Although soils may contain mineral particles of literally any size, from nearly microscopic clay to visible bits of rock (sand), they are usually classified into three categories based on the size, shape, and behavior of the particles predominating: *clay, silt,* and *sand*. *Clay* particles are smallest. Thin and flat, they pack tightly together and restrict the movement of water, air, and even a plant's roots through the soil. This density makes watering dried-out clay soils extremely difficult. The water runs over the clay, down the cracks, and away. Ironically, clay is rich in essential plant nutrients but the inability of water and air to move evenly in and out inhibits the processes by which these nutrients are released to the plants. Of all the more or less pure types of soil, heavy clays are the worst for containers; the small volume possible in containers will not permit the great deal of modification and special care they require, even in a field. Drainage, the single most critical factor in container gardening, is virtually nonexistent in clay.

Silt particles are medium size, and they provide a fairly good balance of water absorption, retention, and drainage, air spaces, and conditions suitable for the decomposition of organic matter, so important in natural soils. It provides few nutrients, however, and you are unlikely to find it, anyway, unless you live near the mouth of a river.

The largest soil particles are *sand*. Because they are large and round, sand particles lie loosely without packing together. Sand is not a very good source of minerals, and it permits such rapid movement of water that added nutrients are flushed too quickly through the soil to be picked up by the plants.

Soils, fortunately, rarely consist of a single type of particle. Most contain particles of many sizes, with one of the characteristic types predominating. A good soil contains such a balanced mixture of clay, silt, and sand that it drains well yet retains moisture, provides good physical support for trees and other tall plants yet permits tiny roots and tender new growth to penetrate freely. Such an ideal soil is called *loam*, and it is the goal of all soil improvement and the model for mixing synthetic soils.

Chemical balance—All soils can be described in terms of their acidity or alkalinity as well as by their physical characteristics. The chemical balance generally affects the consistency of the soil, the availability of nutrients, and, in organic soils at least, the presence and activity level of microorganisms. It also determines which plants will grow.

Chemical balance is measured on a pH scale, which runs from 1 to 14; 7 is neutral. A pH reading below 7 indicates that the soil is sour, or acid; above, that it is sweet, or alkaline (sometimes referred to as "base" or "basic"). By mixing your own soil from standard components, you can tailor the chemical balance to suit the plants growing in it. The majority of popular garden plants do best when the pH is between 6 and 7.5 but a few, azaleas, heather, and blueberries, for example, prefer 4.5 to 6. Many other plants cannot grow in such acid soils, though vegetables, yews, and some flowers thrive in the mildly acid range of 6 to 6.5. Certain humuses—such as oak leaves (composted) and some types of peat moss—have an

acidifying effect on soil. Lime, in the form of ground limestone or, even better, hydrated lime with about 75 percent calcium, can be used to sweeten an acid soil. Naturally acid soils tend to be high in organic matter and in levels of biological activity.

In alkaline soils, on the other hand, many nutrients are simply unavailable—either not present at all, or locked into stable compounds, hence inaccessible to the plants. Alkaline soils need major rebuilding, something you should never attempt (or need to do) in a container.

Soil temperature—The temperature of the soil is usually a reflection of air temperature, but it is also influenced by mulches and position relative to the sun. Soil temperature is important for several reasons. Seeds are programmed to germinate, grow, flower, and fruit within specific temperature ranges and durations; some seeds (beans, for instance) will simply rot in cold soil. In fact, biological activity is generally keyed to temperature levels. Consequently, not only germination but other processes within the plant—the diffusion of nutrient solution from cell to cell and thus transpiration, for example—may be retarded in cold soil. Advice to water plants with tepid water is based on such considerations as these, although the effects of using cold water (except for sensitive tropical houseplants) may be exaggerated. Extremely hot soil, on the other hand, can cause an overload; the plant may go into shock, its leaves wilt, and all processes stop.

Roof garden container soils—Soils used on the roof should be more moisture-retentive than ordinary garden soils and exceptionally well drained. Even on a strong concrete roof they should be light in weight, if only for ease of mixing and handling. Roof garden soils must also drain rapidly. Plants require air to absorb and utilize nutrients from the soil. Most natural soils, even those which drain adequately in a field, are likely to become compacted in a container, thus restricting the passage of air. Many of the forces which loosen and separate soil particles in the ground—earthworms, biological activity (the continuous decomposition and replacement of humus)—are curtailed or nonexistent in the restricted space of the container. Furthermore, the high-efficiency, low-bulk synthetic fertilizers commonly used in containers, so desirable in some respects, fail to aerate the soil as organic supplements would.

A well-drained soil encourages water to penetrate evenly through the entire container, which is necessary for the health of the plant. If the soil doesn't drain properly the container may appear to be well watered when only a shallow layer at the top is actually wet. Because roots cannot penetrate dry soil, they extend through only the moist upper layer. The rest of the space is wasted, and the plant needs extra watering and fertilizing because of it. Such shallow roots make it easy for aggressive weeds (even on the roof) to steal what water and nutrients are available, and make weeding and cultivation difficult, since you will need to avoid damaging the fragile roots lying just beneath the top of the soil.

Good drainage also helps prevent overfeeding or fertilizer burn, most likely in a badly drained, shallowly watered container. It can even happen in containers which have received no fertilizers, if the mineral nutrients extracted from soil particles, added earlier as fertilizer or accumulated from any other source, dissolve in soil water in larger densities than needed by the plant. If drainage is good, the excess passes out of the container; if it is poor, the nutrient salts will remain in the soil, subsequently increasing the concentration of the solution around the plant's roots. Several of the minerals required in minute quantities for growth are toxic in higher concentrations. Harmful accumulations are unlikely in a fast-draining soil mixture, in which excesses are flushed through and out of the container during regular waterings.

Moisture retention is as important as good drainage for most plants, particularly in a hot, windy roof garden. If water simply rushes through the container, mineral nutrients will not remain where the plant's roots can collect them, and fragile but important root hairs are likely to die if they dry out.

Organic container soil mixtures—If you decide to use a more or less natural soil for your roof garden, it is better to use commercial topsoil than soil collected from a garden as the base of the mixture. It should also include builder's (not beach) sand—to lighten the soil and improve drainage—and leaf

mold, compost, or other biologically active humus—to improve moisture retention. The use of perlite or vermiculite in place of sand will further improve drainage and moisture retention, and make the mixture lighter. The proportions of topsoil, sand, and humus should be roughly equal by volume, though at times humus may form 50 percent of the mixture to compensate for its decomposition. The proportion of humus should never fall much below one-third, for on it depend not only the critical moisture balance but also the nourishment of your plants. This combination is an organic soil mixture. It is a light, faster-draining version of what you might achieve by improving the soil in a garden, and it will function as naturally as a container soil can. It is relatively heavy, however, thanks to the use of topsoil and sand, and it may be a source of disease, particularly if you use garden soil.

Lightweight container soil mixtures—A half-and-half mixture of vermiculite or perlite and moist, finely milled dark sphagnum moss makes an excellent container soil for the roof. (Dark peat is less likely to be strongly acid than the yellow or tan varieties, which should be reserved for acid-loving plants.) Horticulturally clean finely chipped bark or sawdust with nitrogen added, available from reliable nurseries and garden centers, can be substituted for the peat moss. Bone meal, dry fertilizers, or time-release fertilizers may be worked into this mixture, though I prefer to wait and use liquid solutions as the plants need them. These materials are relatively economical in bulk (avoid the little packages at the dime store; nurseries offer 2- and 4-cubic-yard bales), especially compared to the cost of ready-made lightweight mixes, which have various forms of fertilizer included.

Warning: Avoid inhaling the dust released when mixing any soil components, no matter how natural they are or harmless they seem. Cover your nose with a handkerchief or special mask (sold in hardware stores for use in wood- and metalworking shops). Any particle fine enough to enter and stay in your lungs will do them no good.

Supplementing container soils—All container soils require supplementation. Even the best organic soils are likely to develop deficiencies in nitrogen and other readily soluble elements in a container. This necessary supplementation, however, can take several forms.

Organic fertilizers or supplements are animal and vegetable substances taken almost unaltered from nature. They include, among many, manure (well rotted before use), bone meal, dried blood, processed sewage sludge, and wood ashes. Organic fertilizers supplement the soil as they did before modern technology enabled gardeners to diagnose the lack of a specific mineral and to replace it. For long-term ground-level gardens, organic fertilizers are a necessity—they aerate and condition the soil, rather than just lie in it. Organic fertilizers provide nutrients indirectly, as nature does, and in the process add bulk and microorganisms which improve texture, water retention, and aeration (or tilth). They tend to work slowly and steadily, reducing the likelihood of fertilizer damage and of uneven growth resulting from fluctuating levels of required nutrients. Because they are less pure (less refined), organic supplements are also good sources of secondary and trace elements, which are not always available from manufactured fertilizers.

The major obstacle to using organic fertilizers in containers is their inefficiency. Most are needed in bulk, and may demand more space and time than are available to many roof gardeners. However, it is almost always useful to add rotted manure, compost, and bone meal to organic container soils, and bone meal is a useful additive for any soils used for bulbs and other perennial plants. Another disadvantage to organic supplements is that their composition varies, depending on their source. It is difficult for a gardener in the city to know, for example, just what, besides nitrogen, an anonymous manure is likely to supply, though the farmer will know exactly what the cow who contributed it had been eating. Furthermore, some organic materials are in short supply, especially in cities, far from the farms where they originated and are primarily used.

Synthetic or chemical fertilizers are the products of technology. They are formulated to supply plants with one or several of the essential elements required for growth, in direct or nearly direct form. Because most nutrients are required in minute quantities, the elements are usually packaged with inert extenders, facilitating spreading and mixing the fertilizers evenly into the soil.

A "complete" fertilizer, oddly, is one which contains the big three nutrients—nitrogen (N), phosphorus (P), and potassium (K)—but probably only those. Fertilizers come in different formulas (or N-P-K ratios), such as 0-15-30, 5-10-10, or 4-8-4, designed to suit different groups of plants. The total of the three figures (45, 25, or 16 in the examples given) tells you what percentage of the package contents is fertilizer; if you subtract that figure from 100, you will know the percentage of inert extender (55, 75, or 84 in the examples given). The directions for use will generally reflect the ratio of active to inactive ingredients; low-potency fertilizers will require larger doses per application than high ones. As the concentration of active components increases, so does the likelihood of overfertilizing; therefore, in general, low-efficiency fertilizers are recommended for plants growing in containers.

Chemical fertilizers are prepared as powders, for dry application, which is the messiest, bulkiest, and cheapest form; soluble granules, for dissolving and administering in water; and time-release beads, for incorporation into the soil when mixing it or worked into soil already in a container, which is the cleanest, most convenient, and most expensive form. You can probably ignore the differences in costs of the different forms of fertilizer, as few roof gardens are large enough to need more than a few dollars' worth each season, but convenience is an important consideration. Personally, I hate the powders. They're a mess to keep, the bags leak even before they're opened, they absorb moisture during storage and turn into bricks, they blow around when you try to use them, and the stuff gets on the leaves and kills them. The time-release beads, on the other hand, are convenient to store and use, but they have serious drawbacks when used in the well-drained containers so necessary on the roof. I have used 3M's Precise for tomatoes, but the tiny beads seem to have been washed through the soil and eventually out of the container without dissolving and releasing nutrients for the plants. I think a denser soil—one based on topsoil, for instance—or a brand which comes in larger pellets (like Osmacote) might work. I prefer to use soluble granules as they not only store and handle easily but give the best control of any type of fertilizer. Whichever form you use, look for fertilizers which provide both secondary and trace elements, not merely the big three; an analysis of the contents appears on the package of every fertilizer.

Always use fertilizers at half or quarter strength, twice or three times as often as recommended, to provide even levels of nutrients throughout the growing season, and always water containers from the top until water drains from the bottom, to wash any precipitated nutrient salts out of the container.

THE ATMOSPHERE

The atmosphere supports a plant's stems and leaves much as the soil supports its roots. The atmosphere's condition—essentially, its temperature, amount of moisture, and degree of movement or wind—is referred to as weather or climate. The climate changes daily as well as seasonally, and it places practical limits on the plants which will grow on your roof without greenhouses or other special facilities. Unlike soil, which can be mixed and supplemented to fulfill almost any needs, you cannot really change your climate, though its effects on your plants can be moderated, especially in a container garden. No garden—on the roof or on the ground—has a perfect climate for every plant all the time but if you understand how climate affects plants, you will be able to make the most of the garden you have.

Temperature—Air temperature largely determines soil temperature, and it would be important for that reason if there were no other. It also seems to be part of the plant's information system—along with the quality, angle, and duration of light—which triggers blooming, fruiting, dormancy, and death. Plants are able to absorb and use nutrients most efficiently when the soil and air are within a particular range of temperatures, but

this ideal may vary radically from plant to plant. Air temperature determines humidity, since cool air is able to hold less moisture than warm air, and thus influences the rate of transpiration. If cold soil temperatures are accompanied by dry air (typical of winter climates), transpiration is increased (even during dormancy) while root absorption is reduced, sometimes causing the foliage to die back. (This is often referred to as winter scorch, sunburn, or freezing damage, though these terms are inaccurate.) A worse problem will occur if the water held in the soil freezes while the plant is growing actively. This can happen if you apply fertilizer late or try to garden under city street lights so the plant is fooled into growing too late in the season or if there is an early or late frost which catches the plant by surprise. Water expands as it freezes, disrupting soil particles and scraping or breaking root hairs and the fragile tips of feeder roots, perhaps even shoving the plant up out of the soil. If the plant is dormant, this heaving, as it is often called, will be less damaging, but it is never desirable. Preventing it is one of the main reasons for insulating containers of shrubs, perennials, and bulbs.

The other extreme, all too likely on an unshaded roof, is that the soil can become too hot, especially in an uninsulated, dark-colored container (metal, particularly, which conducts heat well). Such a build-up of heat will prevent the plant from taking nutrients and water in through its roots, then the water is likely to evaporate, and the plant will finally wilt and perhaps die. In the worst cases, tissues can actually be destroyed by soil heat.

Moisture—Most plants like high humidity and regular doses of water, especially during periods of active growth, and even—though less—during dormancy. Water is critically needed for plant growth for many reasons. To begin with, plant tissues are 90 percent water. Furthermore, water contains the oxygen necessary for fuel conversion in the plant, and it is the medium by which nutrients are absorbed by plants from soil-held solutions, controlling the transfer of nutrients and manufactured food within the plant by diffusion from cell to cell. Besides causing the obvious problems of wet, compacted soil and moist, disease-prone foliage, heavy rain for several days can leach the most soluble nutrients (particularly nitrogen) from the soil and out of the container.

Wind—Moving air is generally good for your garden. It assists transpiration by reducing humidity around the plants, and discourages fungal diseases which depend on still, moist air to become established. Wind pollinates many non-flowering plants, and helps to moderate temperature, by mixing the air in your garden with other (probably cooler) air from adjacent areas. Few roofs lack moving air, fortunately, since it is difficult and expensive to create.

5

Every Garden Needs Plants. . .

BUYING SEEDS AND TRANSPLANTS

You could create an entire roof garden from seeds and cuttings. It might take years to achieve a finished garden, with contrasting sizes and varieties of plants, but your cash outlay would be small and you would have the satisfaction of a job well done. On the other hand, you could purchase mature specimens and have a nearly instant garden. The plants in most roof gardens are assembled gradually from a variety of sources. Vegetables and flowers may be started from seeds (or bulbs), or purchased as starter plants. Woody vines, shrubs, and trees are usually bought either as young transplants or as older specimens, though some—particularly the willows—can be rooted from cuttings.

Beginning plants from seed can be an arduous process. The first year I gardened in the city, every warm nook and corner in our apartment held its makeshift germination chamber. Coping with dogs, cat, and family members who feel displaced by all the blown-up plastic bags for the several weeks needed to produce healthy plants ready for the garden can be a poor beginning to your summer garden (as it was to mine). Since I can't resist baby plants and the chance to make an early jump on spring, I still grow a few vegetables from seed each year, restraining myself to unusual varieties—like midgets, snow peas, or purple-podded beans—not available as starter plants at the nursery.

Seeds are usually inexpensive, with small fluc-

tuations in price from year to year reflecting crop yields and other market variables. The cost of beginning from seed cannot be reckoned so easily, however, as each packet—even the smallest—is likely to contain more than you need, even after allowing for a certain loss from germination failure and thinning. You must also add the price of germinating and transplanting materials, and possibly lights or heaters for some plants. Most gardeners who begin with purchased plants usually start a few from seed the following year, either to have special varieties or because of increased confidence in their gardening abilities. Beginning with seeds is exciting as well as economical. Any additional trouble can often be offset by a reduction in scale—you can have a smaller garden and take more pleasure in it.

On the other hand, while you do pay for convenience when you buy plants (or anything, for that matter), it is often worth paying for, particularly when establishing a new garden. Everything takes a little more time than envisioned, and problems can arise with even the best planned garden. Using as many starter plants as you can find or afford will free you to handle unexpected chores. You can buy small flats from a local nursery, particularly if you want just one or two of a kind. While you may not find every variety you like, there will be some—like pansies and other biennials—generally available only as plants. Today, most nurseries offer mixed flats—two each of three different tomatoes or marigolds, for example, or even a salad mix of lettuce, peppers, chives, celery, and tomatoes—in recognition of the needs of new gardeners and small city gardens. Though more costly than seeds, starter plants are still relatively inexpensive; a small flat of six or eight plants might cost ninety-eight cents, and if they are healthy, all can be expected to mature. Larger flats work out to a lower per-plant cost, so it is worth your while to grow more or to share with another gardener. Depending on your source, however, buying already started plants can introduce problems—insects, for one. The best nursery may harbor aphids or whitefly (as may the best garden), but it is foolish to assist an already awe-inspiring transport system by bringing the pests home. Secondly, your supplier may offer only a limited variety of started plants. While a good seed house will have a dozen varieties of tomatoes or lettuce, for example, a local nursery may have only one or two types of each.

The woody plants—perennial vines, shrubs, and trees—are virtually always bought as plants, although some, such as the readily rooted willows just mentioned, can be propagated from cuttings or layering, and are well worth experimenting with, at least once your garden is established. You can even grow woody plants from seed, available from a few specialty nurseries, but germination of these seeds usually requires exceptional patience and skill.

Where to Buy

Seeds and plants are sold everywhere—in nurseries, of course, but also at hardware, variety, and grocery stores, at florists and even at flea markets and gas stations. There are also more mail-order houses than can be listed. How do you decide where to buy?

A local grower is the best place, at least for woody plants, and any other local nursery is a good second choice. The plants you buy will have a short trip home, which is good for them, and you can establish a relationship with the owners, which can be invaluable for you, as most growers and nursery operators know not only all about the plants they sell but about gardening in general as well. The plants should also be well adapted to your climate, as they have been chosen—possibly even grown—for the region. A local outlet is convenient—you can go to the nursery for planning and estimating costs before committing yourself to any purchases, and you can often have the nursery planner come to your roof for a consultation (for a small fee, usually credited to later purchases) if you feel out of your depth, if your roof offers special problems, or if you just want professional advice.

On the other hand, a local nursery may be limited. While it will undoubtedly feature the popular gardening standards of your area, some of these plants will be unsuitable for the restricted scale of the roof garden, while others, perhaps slower to sell, might appeal to you if they were offered. Mail-order seed and plant sellers offer a wider selection, although some may specialize—in herbs, orchids, fruit trees, or succulents, for example. There can be problems with buying by mail, however. Plants may fail to arrive altogether, though that is rare in my experience. Sometimes a plant will arrive dead or dying, usually because of mishandling in transit, or a plant may arrive at the wrong time, though that is now usually controlled very reliably by computers. Whatever the cause of the difficulty, most dealers guarantee their mail-order sales and replace the plants, at the proper time. Many gardeners feel that a mail-order plant differs radically from its description in the catalog, and certainly some of the descriptions are high-flown and florid, but you can guard against most of these disappointments by visualizing a 2-inch pot or an 18-inch plant, as described in the factual portion of the text, before you order it. While catalog illustrations portray what a plant may become, the descriptions usually tell you what the nursery is actually shipping.

Sophisticated in-city plant stores usually specialize in houseplants and exotica, but a few carry herbs, starter vegetables and flowers, and medium-to-large plants you can grow on the roof in the summer, if not year-round. Some specialize in roof and terrace gardens. Do not confuse these modern plant stores with flower shops offering a sideline of living plants; many plant stores provide consulting and designing services and garden maintenance, as well as plants, for those too busy (or too overwhelmed) to do their own, all for a fee which may be credited to subsequent plant

This "walkout" is part of City University of New York's Hunter College. It is a student facility designed for between-class relaxation and visual pleasure.

A clay pot of hybrid impatiens highlights a striking view of lower Manhattan.

This view of residential city buildings shows two gardens, both fairly traditional and formal, more for passive enjoyment than working in.

A small city terrace is a convenient place for a greenhouse; the floor above is a pleasant, easy-to-care-for retreat, featuring upright shrubs, Virginia creeper, and ivy.

City dwellers often try to extend their living space with gardens such as this one, using shrubs and pots of annuals for low upkeep.

Rooftop architecture makes a dramatic frame for a garden. Here climbing vines have been trained up some structures and over others.

Watertowers, stairwells, and other rooftop structures are typical of many older city buildings. Although they often cause design problems, they also help to create intimacy in a roof garden.

This tiny enclosed rooftop is further protected by many small trees and shrubs to provide privacy for reading and sunbathing in the heart of the city.

Russian olive (*Eleagnus angustifolia*), shown here in a half barrel, is an excellent roof garden plant. Annuals—petunias, dusty miller, and basil—help hide the inevitable bare space near the soil.

Holly will grow in a container, for a while at least. This young one is sparse, so its owner has filled in with summer annuals—red salvia, white petunias, and sweet alyssum.

purchases. If the staff is competent, plant stores are reliable sources, although they tend to emphasize a relatively expensive package of plant-plus-service, rather than the simple sale of a wide variety of plants alone.

There are many other places to buy plants, some of them unorthodox. Virtually every seasoned gardener can tell of finding a long sought-after, rare, or otherwise distinguished specimen at a flea market, PTA sale, or in the dime store. Certainly plant sales by botanical gardens are excellent sources, although most of the plants will be traditional, purchased for the sale, rather than the unusual plants normally displayed. The best buys at such sales are plants from a garden club, which will not only likely be unusual, but accompanied by excellent cultural information. Plant societies often have exchange programs for their members, and they are among the best plant sources, if you are primarily interested in one type of plant, since each society specializes.

Variety stores usually carry only the most obvious, hard-to-kill houseplants (which they proceed to test by placing them in the darkest corner, where they remain, unwatered and unexamined, until sold), but some stores (not chains—individual outlets) take better care of plants than others. It seems to depend on the staff. In any event, I don't really recommend variety stores; it's just that there are those occasional finds that make considering them worthwhile, and for some gardeners, they are the only ready source of live plants. You can certainly buy seeds in variety stores, of course, as well as in many other unlikely places. Most of the brands are reliable—in fact, it seems that one or two seed companies supply all the outlets—but there may be a lack of choice, and you should be careful to check that the seed packet bears this year's date. The best selection of seeds comes from large mail-order seed houses, but you must think a month or two ahead to buy from them.

What to Look For

No matter what the source, you should take home only strong, healthy, well-grown plants. You *can* save a sinking plant, rescue one debili-

tated by red spider, prune and salvage a leggy plant grown in poor light, but why should you? Such a plant may never recover, particularly if it is an annual, with just a few short weeks to live, and the same amount of effort lavished on already healthy plants could generate phenomenal blossoms or an impressive yield. Meanwhile, depending on what's wrong with it, one sickly plant could infect others in your garden.

A healthy plant usually looks healthy. Its leaves are intact and the appropriate color, its stems are turgid, not limp from lack of cellular moisture, and the internodes are the proper length for the species and variety. A plant with missing or severely damaged leaves, floppy stems, or bleached or stained foliage has undergone (or is undergoing) trauma or illness. A healthy plant also has a healthy, strong root system. It is neither possible nor necessarily good for the plant to expose the root system of every prospective purchase, but root damage shows up in the foliage and flowers. Plants with brown or limp stems and leaves should always be avoided, and you should think twice about any plant that is shedding blossoms, at least in quantity. Shrubs and trees, even dwarfs, need extensive root systems to survive, especially in containers on the roof. Roots actually bind the soil, so you can tell something about a plant's condition by feeling the soil around the roots; it should be firm but not compacted. If you do unpot the plant, most of the soil should be bound to the roots, not loose in the container. Always buy labeled plants; related but drastically different varieties may resemble each other when young—a bushy, spreading shrub may look like a compact one when both are in 3-inch pots, and you will have wasted a lot of time and energy by the time you discover the difference.

Avoid insects, or at least avoid plants with blatant signs of infestation. A well-run nursery or plant shop may have a few pests around, especially if it is run on organic principles, but any plant with *obvious* mealybug, scale, whitefly, or red spider should be avoided. By the time these pests are visible, they are nearly impossible to get rid of, especially in combination with the trauma of moving the plant to your roof, without seriously impairing the plant's development. You ought to be thinking of your other plants, as well, and not import extra pests to your garden, where they will appear anyway in their own good time.

Seeds have to be taken more or less at face value. You can easily compare the guaranteed germination rate of one brand to another (assuming it is given), and make sure the package is dated for this year, not last. But, in my experience, most seeds are essentially reliable and, unless you have contradictory experience, may be taken as described. Some packets have very cursory descriptions, although seed catalogs are generally thorough in giving the size and form of the mature plant, days to maturity, and proper planting depth and spacing. Hybrids have been created to produce extraordinary results particularly among vegetables—unusual color or size, resistance to disease, earlier maturation date, or improved yields—and something has been given up to achieve these effects. You may very well be content with the less expensive old-fashioned varieties. If you use pasteurized ("sterilized") soil or soil substitutes, in a clean container, the diseases which plague commercial growers are extremely unlikely on your roof, and you need not buy hybrids with resistance to these diseases unless you also prefer them for other reasons. Unless you are preserving, you should avoid the market varieties of vegetables and fruits, which mature during a short time span, and instead choose varieties with a long yield time. Read catalog and package descriptions carefully. In general they can be counted on to help you avoid the sprawling, long-stemmed, heavy-fruited varieties which need more space and support than you and your roof can offer conveniently, but the hard facts may be dribbled through a sea of prose.

Choosing plants need not be mysterious, but it is not an absolutely cut-and-dried process either. When choosing annuals—flowers and vegetables—you can certainly afford to experiment, but even more permanent plants should be viewed from a flexible point of view.

TREES, SHRUBS, AND VINES

It is always best to choose the larger woody plants first when beginning a garden. These are the plants you rely on to integrate your garden and the buildings and other structures around it, and to create a stage or framework for the smaller, more colorful plants to be planted later. Larger plants require more planning. They are harder to move and less likely to fit into any random corner than small plants, and they often represent too large an investment for you merely to discard them if they don't work out. Large plants—or even a large grouping of smaller ones—define the gardening areas and introduce order. Until you have trees and vines established, it is difficult to know what and how many other plants are needed. Your garden will look more cohesive and intelligent when you begin at the beginning, with the large plants.

When you purchase a woody vine, shrub, or tree from a grower, you can choose the age (thus the size) and, usually, the form in which it will be delivered. Roots may be bare (customary for dormant roses and other shrubs); with their ball of soil, wrapped in burlap, usually called "B & B" for "balled and burlapped"; or growing in a container, often a disintegrating cardboard box or tub which may be planted intact (at least in the ground), but occasionally a metal container which must be removed before planting. These conditions vary in usefulness, particularly when you are planting in containers, as you may have to remove even the disintegrating materials at least partially in order to have as much soil as possible around the roots and to prevent the container material from wicking moisture from the soil to the air. When buying plants by mail, specify container-grown shrubs. While they are usually the most costly, they also provide the best protection before you plant. Roses are an exception; as long as they are dormant, they travel bare root very well, and they are cheaper to ship that way. When you are bringing plants home from a local source, you can ask for B & B for economy combined with reasonable safety, but many plants may be available in only one form or another.

As far as the woody plants are concerned, it is always safer to move plants when they are young, while they are small and still actively producing roots and stems. From the strict viewpoint of safety, then, you should always buy "babies"—first- or second-year transplants at the oldest. But, especially when considering a container-grown

All of these plants were collected from the New Hampshire woods, along with their soil. New woods plants spring up from time to time.

specimen (which is something like a big houseplant, after all), which has been acclimated to or comes from outdoors so there will be little shock to the plant, you have little real risk in buying an older plant. At the same time, a few larger and older plants help to define your garden and make it less raw-looking in the beginning. Some plants which appeal to you may be short-lived in a roof garden, so by buying an older plant you can enjoy it during its best period, not its most awkward. One of the bonuses of roof gardening is the restraint on growth imposed by the container. Plants which tend to run wild and take over in the ground, like the ailanthus or honeysuckle, will grow peacefully in a container on the roof. There are rational arguments for buying plants at almost any age—your decision will probably be based as much on taste, gardening style, and the status of your pocketbook as on straightforward horticultural wisdom.

Plant lists are terrible, though a necessary evil in a book of this type. The plants listed on the following pages have been chosen because they are generally tolerant of roof conditions. Sometimes only one variety of a plant is recommended, and sometimes an entire species, and there are undoubtedly many excellent plant possibilities absent from the list. In any event, this (or any) list can be counted on as a guide only and not as a guarantee of success. Throughout this book, plants are listed alphabetically by horticultural or Latin name, to prevent confusion and to provide ease of reference.

Abutilon (flowering maple)—A deciduous shrub with brightly colored flowers and maple-like foliage, with both vining and upright varieties; responds to energetic pinching. Hardy to zone 8.

Ailanthus (tree of heaven, stinkweed)—Fast-growing deciduous tree, often considered a serious pest; resistant to (or thrives on) dirt, dust, smoke, ozone, and other common city pollutants. Though seldom praised, this tree is handsome when restrained, as in a container. Male plants are usually avoided, as they have foul-smelling pods. Hardy to zone 6.

Amelanchier (serviceberry, shadbush, juneberry)—A deciduous tree which, in its smaller varieties, grows nicely on the roof; characterized by

Plant Hardiness Zone Map

The plant hardiness zone map is a useful tool for helping you match your garden with plants—especially woody and other perennial types—capable of growing in it. Hardiness refers to more than a plant's ability to withstand cold. It also takes into account susceptibility to warm or fluctuating winter weather which might cause frost heaving or premature spring growth. A plant may also not be suited to a zone if there is too much light or warmth to bring on a necessary cycle of dormancy. Notwithstanding these qualifications, the hardiness zone system works, as long as you consider the vagaries of your garden. Even country yards have unusual pockets of warmth and cold. Exposed roofs may be subject to winds capable of effectively dropping air temperatures several degrees; on the other hand, cities are generally warmer than less densely populated areas. Furthermore, the heat generated within the building constantly radiates out and upward, making a roof likely to be warmer than nearby places in the open. Taking weekly high and low temperatures at the same places in your garden during the year will help you determine whether your roof is generally warmer or cooler than is normal for your area, and will also define variations from point to point on your roof. Recording the dates of the first and last frost *on your roof* will also help, though you will need to keep records for several years before a reliable pattern can emerge. It is often possible, particularly on a roof, to raise plants successfully from a zone just north or south of your own, particularly if you know your roof is unusually warm or cold. Plants from a distant region, however, cannot be grown without special winter (either warm or cold) facilities.

Ailanthus, the "tree of heaven," which is such a scourge in open gardens, is nicely tamed in this tub.

early, profuse white flowers and bright fall foliage. Some bear an edible purple berry, and self-propagate by stolons or suckers. A romantic and hardy tree, to zone 3.

Araucaria (Norfolk Island pine)—A sturdy needled evergreen tree with orderly tiers of feathery branches, which looks remotely like a pine. Hardy to zone 6 but enjoys being moved in and out with seasons. Likes humidity, filtered sun, and regular watering.

Arctostaphylos Uva-ursi (bearberry)—A trailing evergreen shrub or tree, with large, dry, red berries reputed to be a delicacy for bears. This has a prostrate growth habit which makes it a natural for the top of a parapet or divider. Dislikes lime but is otherwise not too fussy so long as the soil remains moist and loamy. Hardy to zone 3.

Aristolochia (Dutchman's pipe, wild ginger, birthwort)—A deciduous climbing shrub or vine with large heart-shaped leaves and pipe-shaped brown flowers. Give it a large container and

plenty of fertilizer and it will cover almost anything. Tolerates dry soil and shade, but prefers full sun; hardy to zone 7.

Aronia (chokeberry)—An untidy-looking, deciduous shrub with small spring flowers, bright fall leaves, and red winter berries. Hardy to zone 3.

Azalea and *Rhododendron*—Usually evergreen shrubs with flowers of many colors and sizes. Need filtered sun, moist acid soil, rich in organic material, and mulches, or other protection for the shallow-growing surface roots. Prune, if necessary, after blooming, as buds for next year form early. Most hardy to zone 4 or 5.

Berberis (barberry)—Shaggy-growing, usually deciduous shrubs, some with bright autumn leaves. Love full sun, tolerate dry soil, take pruning but can go without it. A good roof garden plant; hardy to zone 4 at least.

Bignonia (cross vine, trumpet flower)—A gaudy

Although not particularly well suited to city conditions or to growing in a container, this yellow globe arborvitae is doing nicely, as is the small azalea in the glazed pot below. These plants are actually on a terrace, so somewhat sheltered from the wind.

and prolific climbing vine with trumpet-shaped flowers and disked clinging tendrils of incredible stick-to-it-iveness, often grown in hanging baskets though it will rapidly cover a wall if you give it full sun, even without the moist soil it prefers. Hardy to zone 6.

Buddleia (butterfly bush, summer lilac)—A compact, semi-evergreen, ornamental flowering shrub, with dense flower clusters. It loves rich, well-drained soil but will grow in almost any mixture in full sun. Hardy to zone 7, but may die back (and regrow) north of zone 5.

Calluna (heather)—A deciduous shrub with short, scale-like leaves and upright flower columns in shades of pink or white. Prefers breezy, sunny places and acid soil with peat or leaf mold, but will grow in most nonlimey soils. Prune each spring; hardy to zone 5.

Caryopteris (blue beard, blue spirea)—A small deciduous shrub with aromatic leaves and clusters of later summer white or blue flowers. Needs light, well-drained soil, and lots of sun; hardy to zone 5 and farther north if protected from winter weather.

Catalpa—A sturdy, profusely flowering, deciduous tree which grows fast, even in poor city conditions. Tolerates almost any soil; the dwarf, *C. bignonioides nana*, is most decorative. Hardy to zone 3.

Cedrus (cedar)—Evergreen coniferous trees with upright cones and clustered needles, likely to do better than most conifers on the roof, as they are relatively pollution resistant though short-lived in a container. Hardy to zone 6 with winter protection.

Celastrus (staff tree, bittersweet)—A deciduous, woody shrub with cheerful red berries which climbs walls and trellises. You may need two varieties to ensure pollination. Tolerates any soil and light conditions; hardy to zone 4.

Celtis occidentalis (hackberry, nettle tree)—Trees with small maroon berries and well-spaced spreading branches which look a little like elms. Fast-growing (to the limit of your container), nearly carefree, dependable, and resistant to wind and pollution. Hardy to zone 2.

Cercis (redbud, Judas tree)—A small tree with red spring "buds" (flowers that look like austere

Sometimes planting a tree, bulbs, and a vine in a single container works wonderfully, as here. It is likely that one of the plants—probably the tree—will take most of the root space.

The twisted hazelnut *(Corylus avellana contorta)* grows slowly in a tub, but, even when very young, its distinctive twisted branches are delightful once its leaves have fallen.

sweet peas), appearing about the same time as dogwood; hardy to zone 3.

Clematis—A climbing or upright deciduous shrub, grown for its bright flowers. Thrives in rich, light soil supplemented with humus, lime, and fertilizers, in a large container. Roots must be deeply covered to protect important near-surface growth, mulched or double-potted to prevent dehydration. Can be difficult, particularly on the roof, but worth taking the trouble. Hardy at least to zone 3.

Cornus (dogwood, cornel, cornelian cherry)— Generally deciduous shrubs or small trees with white (sometimes pink) flowers. There are varieties with variegated foliage, edible cherry-like fruits, pink branches, etc., and all are distinguished. Happy in a roof container, as long as you don't let the soil go dry. Hardy all over the U.S.

Corylus avellana contorta (twisted filbert, hazel; "Harry Lauder's Walking Stick Tree")—A deciduous shrub or small tree with corkscrewing branches, delicate green leaves, and coarsely textured pendent seedpods in the fall. Grows well in most soils, in sun or partial shade; may be susceptible to pollution. Hardy to zone 2.

Cotinus (smoke tree, formerly called *Rhus cotinus*)—A stunning, tasteless-looking tree with great furry flowers and intense autumn foliage. Tolerates any well-drained soil, pollution, and other typical city conditions. Hardy to zone 4.

Cotoneaster—Usually deciduous shrubs, with trailing, upright, and spreading varieties, and leaves ranging in color from dark, shiny green to variegated. Like full sun, any well-drained soil and thrive in containers. Most are ozone resistant, and grow well in polluted gardens. Hardy to zone 4.

Crataegus (haw, hawthorn)—Small deciduous trees with prolific azalea-like, mostly white spring flowers, followed by clusters of red berries. Many varieties with columnar or upright and spreading forms; happy in any soil. Most hardy to zone 2.

Cytisus scoparius (Scotch broom)—A small shrub with erect branches bearing small leaves and flowers along the stems. Hardy to zone 3.

Daphne—A fast-growing shrub, sometimes evergreen, with fragrant star-shaped flowers along

Scotch broom *(Cytisus scoparius)* is unusual in container gardens, though it deserves to be better known. This shrub is as interesting in winter as summer.

the stems. It looks fragile but some varieties will grow nearly everywhere, to zone 3, though it may need winter protection in a container in the North. Likes full sun and loose, well-drained soil, with applications of lime worked in annually and before planting. Note: *Berries, stems, and foliage are poisonous; avoid planting where children and pets may eat them.*

Deutzia—Deciduous shrubs prized for the prolific white spring flowers. Prefer well-drained, humusy soil; hardy to zones 3 or 4, with winter protection in the North. The dwarf *D. gracilis* is a good choice for the roof.

Elaeagnus angustifolia (Russian olive, oleaster)—A small deciduous city tree or shrub with rustly, silvery foliage and occasional spicy-scented tubular flowers. It withstands wind and every other roof condition, in almost any part of the U.S. (to zone 2), and it thrives in full sun and well-drained soil.

Erica (heath)—Evergreen shrubs, with narrow leaves and upright pink flowers which need well-drained acid soil. Most varieties hardy to zone 3.

Euonymus (spindle tree)—Evergreen or deciduous shrubs or small trees of varying growth pattern. Prefer full sun or partial shade and moist, well-drained soil; thrive in cities and near the sea. Strange and wonderful varieties include the cork bark euonymus (*E. alatus monstrosus*) with sculptural, winged branches covered by cork-like bark, and the miniature evergreen bittersweet (*E. kewensis*), a beautiful vine to drape over the parapet or ledge. Hardy to zone 3.

Feijoa (pineapple guava)—An evergreen shrub with edible fruit (not necessarily when grown in a container, however) and oval ornamental leaves. Needs humusy soil and indirect sun. While it will withstand frost, it may do better if brought in during the winter, even in areas where it might survive outside. Hardy to zone 8.

Forsythia (golden bell)—An easy-to-grow shrub, harbinger of spring. Tolerates any soil, smoke, and air pollution. Hardy to zone 2, though it may need winter protection in the North.

Gramineae (grasses)—Decorative grasses, often called architectural or ornamental grasses—including pampas grass (*Cortaderia*), bamboo (*Bambusa*), quake grass (*Bromus brizaeformis*), Job's tears (*Coix*), rabbit's tail (*Lagurus*), canary grass (*Phalaris*), and one or two varieties of corn (*Zea*)—which are beautiful grown in a container. Most are perennial in warm climates but will grow as annuals (or indoor-outdoor plants) over most of the U.S.

Grass-like shrubs (see *Nandina, Cytisus scoparius*)

Hamamelis (witch hazel)—A winter-blooming deciduous shrub, of interest for the year-round garden particularly. Strangely contorted petals, fragrant spidery flowers. At least one variety is hardy everywhere to zone 2 or 3.

Hedera (ivy)—A fast-growing, long-lasting evergreen shrub with many varieties. Likes cool, moist locations, shade, and a wall (of almost any nonwooden material) to climb on, but will tolerate dryness and hanging in a basket. Hardy to zone 4. Note: *The entire ivy plant is poisonous to eat, and some people may also develop skin reactions after pruning it.*

Humulus (hop)—Fast-growing perennial vine, source of beer-making hop, will cover 10 to 20 feet in a season even in a container. The most nearly decorative form is *H. Japonicus variegatus*. Certainly hardy to zone 7, perhaps farther north with

Russian olive *(Elaeagnus angustifolia)* is a great city shrub. This one has just been planted.

protection. Note: *Handling hop plants may cause allergic skin reactions in some people.*

Hydrangea (snowball)—Deciduous shrubs with large clusters of flowers, available in many varieties; all need moist soil but tolerate other conditions well, including containers, city air, and proximity to the sea. Hardy to zone 2 or 3. Note: *Hydrangeas are poisonous under certain conditions; they should not be grown where curious toddlers or pets can eat them.*

Juniperus (juniper)—Trees with varied foliage which thrive all over the country (to zone 1); need well-drained light soil and lots of sun. The spreading varieties sold as ground covers are excellent on the roof because of their indifference to wind and dryness, and the upright varieties make good windbreaks. Note: *Juniper needles and sap are poisonous to eat.*

Kerria—A tough deciduous shrub with beautiful yellow, rose-like flowers which will grow happily in any well-drained soil and partial shade. Hardy to zone 3, but needs shelter everywhere from heavy wind.

Kolkwitzia (beauty bush)—A reliable deciduous shrub with profuse pink flowers. Needs a relatively large container but endures drought and wind. Hardy to zone 3.

Lagerstroemia (crape myrtle)—Another beautiful shrub, with clustered flowers having fringed, pastel petals. Hardy to zone 5. Needs full sun to ensure blooming but during the first two years in a container it may not bloom.

Laurus (laurel, sweet bay)—The laurel has stiff aromatic leaves used for cooking. Tolerates abuse, including heavy pruning, but needs moist, loamy soil. The laurel is perennial, at least in the South (hardy to zone 6), but in the North it tolerates neither life in a heated apartment nor winter outdoors. On the roof laurels can survive if grouped, wrapped, and sheltered to keep the temperature a few degrees above freezing, as long as the soil does not dry out. They are well worth the trouble.

Ligustrum (privet)—A deciduous shrub much used for hedges in the Northeast. An excellent screen for sun, it thrives despite pollution and adapts to life at the shore; it likes sun, shade, and any soil. Privet is evergreen as far north as New York City (hardy from zone 3 to 7). A single specimen in a tub looks distinctive, probably because we are accustomed to seeing privets lined up in a row. Note: *Both berries and leaves are poisonous to eat.*

Lilac (see *Syringa*)

Lonicera (honeysuckle)—A deciduous climber with drooping, heavily scented cylindrical flowers appearing at various times of the summer and, in some varieties, lasting until fall. Prefers a moist, well-drained loam; hardy to zone 3. Although it has a tendency to become rampant in the ground, honeysuckle is nicely restrained by growing in a container.

Mahonia (holly grape, holly barberry, Oregon grape)—A low-growing evergreen shrub with grape-like berries, holly-shaped, shiny spiny leaves, and attractive flowers. Needs protection from wind and direct sun all year; most are hardy to zone 3 or 4.

Malus (flowering crabapple)—Fruit trees grown essentially for their flowers. Although related to flowering cherries, crabs are tougher, more tolerant of unusual conditions, and they come in more patterns of growth and foliage colors than the cherries. The weeping forms are among the most beautiful small weeping trees, and there are also slender upright varieties for narrow spaces. They will grow cheerfully in almost any soil as long as it is well drained; hardy to zone 2.

Nandina (heavenly or sacred bamboo)—An evergreen shrub (not a true bamboo) which is hardy year-round as far north as zone 6. Grows slowly, needs good light and a rich, loamy, moist soil. The reed-like stalks whisper graciously in the wind, creating distracting white noise.

Nerium (oleander)—Evergreen shrubs commonly grown in tubs in the North (above zone 7), where they are not hardy. Oleanders are easy to grow. They seem almost to thrive on neglect (which does not include drying out), but do need winter storage at a moist 40°F. Note: *All parts of oleander are poisonous, perhaps fatal, if eaten. Do not plant oleander if small children or pets can possibly eat it. It may also cause dermatitis in sensitive individuals.*

Parthenocissus (Boston ivy, ampelopsis, Virginia creeper)—A handsome, deciduous, ivy-like vine which will climb almost anything in almost any

The dramatic Virginia creeper form of *Parthenocissus* will happily grow to cover this wall. In this picture it is being trained by means of patented holding devices, available from good garden centers.

direction from almost any soil though it may need a little help in the beginning. Some varieties are hardy to zone 2.

Philadelphus (mock orange)—Deciduous shrubs with cream or white flowers with delicate, persistent fragrance. Will grow in any good, well-drained soil, likes sun, and endures city conditions. Prune after flowering. Hardy to zone 4 (and some varieties farther north).

Phyllostachys—Bamboo-like shrubs which take readily to growth in tubs. They grow densely enough to serve as a visual screen, are easy to care for, and most are hardy to zone 5.

Pinus (pine)—A needled evergreen tree with many growth habits and sizes. Most adaptable of the conifers but should be obtained as a young transplant or container-grown specimen. Prefers well-drained sandy loam but will accept most soils if not too wet; loves light. The jack pine (*P. banksiana*) is tough and lovable; does well in dry soils and wind. The mugho pine is low-growing, sturdy, and does well in containers; and the Japanese black pine (*P. thunbergi*) tolerates both

city and seaside conditions. Pines are valuable for the roof but some are susceptible to pollution damage, particularly from ozone and sulfur dioxide. Note: *Both the needles and the sap may cause digestive upsets if eaten.*

Platanus (Plane, sycamore)—Densely leafed deciduous trees with maple-like foliage. One variety, the London plane tree, tolerates city conditions well, and it is thus somewhat overused, but, restrained in a container, it is handsome. Hardy to zone 3.

Populus (poplar, aspen, cottonwood)—Deciduous trees with thick, slender leaves. They tend to overrun ground-level gardens but are nicely restrained in a container, where they may need occasional root pruning. (This is not an ideal container tree, but one worth trying. I know a small American aspen—*P. tremuloides*—growing in a New York City roof garden, and it is incredibly beautiful.) Hardy to zone 2.

Pyracantha (firethorn)—A sturdy evergreen shrub with berries which last through the winter. Tolerates dry soil and loves sun; enjoys pruning and will grow in containers, up a wall, across a

This spruce and the soil it grows in were collected in the country. The wild plants (or weeds), including the ubiquitous lamb's-quarters (center), are all volunteers, having been brought in in the soil.

This casual collection of native Northeastern plants includes, unusually, a tub of Hosta (in the lower right-hand corner) and oxalis (in the trash can at the left). Other plants include iris, a small evergreen, Virginia creeper, and a rose.

frame, or anywhere. Hardy to zone 6 (a few to zone 4 or 5).

Rhododendron (see *Azalea*)

Robinia pseudo-acacia (black locust, false acacia)—Very beautiful deciduous trees, with drooping open foliage and flower clusters followed by seedpods. Hardy to zone 3; tolerate any dry soil and resist smoke, wind, and other city conditions.

Rosa (rose)—Well-known deciduous shrubs grown for their flowers, which take hundreds of sizes, forms, and colors, with and without the familiar scent. Supposedly high-maintenance plants, my hybrid climbers grow in a plastic bucket and climb all over the railing while I do very little to care for them. The subject of many good books and widely diverse opinions—too many for this list.

Salix (willow)—Fast-growing deciduous trees which tend to get brittle as they age, but which grow fast and gracefully in a container. Most varieties need very moist, nearly wet soil. One of the loveliest is the weeping willow *(S. babylonica)*, and it resists city conditions fairly well. It is hardy to zone 3.

This willow has grown for several years in the barrel, which restrains the tree's natural tendency to grow rampantly.

Sorbus (ash)—Graceful deciduous trees with lacy leaves and clusters of white or orange berries in the fall and white flowers in the spring. Hardy to zone 3.

Spiraea (spirea)—Small deciduous shrubs with profuse small flowers on arched stalks. Love sun and rich, moist, loamy soil but will endure most conditions. Hardy to zone 3. The bridal wreath variety *(S. vanhouttei)* is especially resistant to smoke, soot, and other pollution.

Syringa (lilac)—Shrubs prized for their lovely, drooping, scented flower clusters which appear in the spring. Several varieties can be container grown; tolerate any soil but thrive in rich, well-drained soil and good sun. Some varieties are susceptible to urban pollution. Hardy to zone 3, and the common lilac *(S. vulgaris)* to zone 2.

Tamarix (tamarisk)—A deciduous shrub with long branches, small heath-like leaves and small flowers. A good windbreak, and it tolerates city and seaside conditions. Hardy to zone 7.

Taxus (yew)—Useful evergreen shrubs or trees of many shapes and growth patterns; love moist,

Flowering vines can be trained onto almost any structure. A denser planting would cover the support—unnecessary here, as it is so attractive.

loamy soil but will grow in almost any good humusy soil as long as it is not highly acid or compacted. Hardy to zone 3. Note: *The leaves are poisonous if eaten, having a depressant action on the heart.*

Thuja (arborvitae)—Evergreen trees which take a wide variety of forms, including round and columnar, and several colors. Thrive in cool air and a protected location, in moist loam or sandy soil. They grow slowly and hate temperature extremes, but they tolerate city conditions fairly well, and are basic to roof gardens. Hardy to zone 4. Note: *Needles, possibly sap, may cause digestive upsets or illness if eaten.*

Tilia (basswood, lime, linden)—Deciduous trees with attractive, sweet-scented spring flowers. Like rich, well-drained soil (hate drying out), but are generally easy-going and tolerant. Hardy to zone 3.

Viburnum (highbush cranberry)—A deciduous or evergreen shrub with compact, bushy foliage. Endures almost any soil, any location, as long as it is not too dry. The highbush cranberry *(V. trilobum)* is decorative, with spring flowers and

The yew was dug from a backyard where it had grown for several years. It seems to do well in this tub, despite perhaps too much sun.

colorful autumn leaves, and it provides edible fruit in the summer. Hardy everywhere.

Weigela—A deciduous shrub with widely spread, pendulous branches and beautiful, trumpet-shaped flowers. It will grow in any soil if it is not too dry. Hardy to zone 3.

Wisteria—Profusely blooming, deciduous shrubs or vines which can be trained up walls or other vertical supports. Wisteria is hardy to zone 3 or 4, and likes rich, moist, loamy soil. Be sure to ask for grafted or blooming stock, or plants may not bloom, or not for several years. Japanese wisteria *(W. floribunda)* and Chinese wisteria *(W. sinensis)* are hardier than others, though smaller.

Xanthoceras (yellow thorn, Chinese flowering chestnut)—A small, deciduous tree or shrub with many large, dramatic, spring-blooming flowers; prefers evenly moist soil. Tolerates city conditions and is hardy to zone 3.

Zelkova serrata (gray bark elm)—A deciduous shrub which resembles a small elm but is more suitable for container growing on a roof. Hardy to zone 3.

FLOWERING ANNUALS

It is a rare garden, on the roof or anywhere, that has no flowers. Many popular varieties grow cheerfully in containers and thrive in rooftop sun, but even if they were difficult to grow, many city gardeners would gladly grow them. For the cost of an average sort of bouquet from a florist you can buy two dozen annuals or a bulb or two to plant in your garden, and have fresh flowers from spring through the fall. Annuals (and bulbs, of course) are the easiest flowers to grow in containers. They, and biennials and perennials grown like annuals, can be grown in several ways, though the easiest is to set out started plants from the nursery. You can also start from seed—either indoors in germination chambers or, once the weather is warm enough, directly in containers.

In contrast to their practice with vegetables, the nurseries always seem to offer every flower variety I ever wanted, so I buy flats of twelve (rarely six) and set them out. Exceptions include such easy to grow, not so easy to transplant favorites as morn-

Easy-to-grow flowers like these *Gloriosa* daisies are cheerful additions to any garden, and most annuals are well adapted to grow in containers.

ing glories, sunflowers, and zinnias, which are best sown directly. I tend to like the old standards—single flowers, not doubles; solid colors, not stripes; old-fashioned yellow, not Kelly green—but I look for hybrids if I need resistance to rooftop conditions or to some disease. If your taste is more sophisticated, the nurseries may not be able to satisfy you, and you will need to start from seed.

There is no reason to segregate the flowers from the other plants in your garden, and many reasons why you should grow them with shrubs, vegetables, and other types of plants. Growing petunias, for example, around the base of a yew or arborvitae conserves container space and provides a contrasting splash of color; morning glories charmingly climb the long stalks of sunflowers; and growing marigolds with beans and other susceptible vegetables is thought to repel the bean beetle. Some flowers, of course, look best alone or in a clump of their own kind, particularly some of the bulbs and ground covers, where the foliage tends to overpower the blossom. By combining a shrub with an upright flower like dwarf hollyhock and a spreader like ageratum, either in a single planter or in several standing together, you can simulate a garden bed.

This picture shows tomatoes, basil, onions, beans, and summer flowers of various types growing happily in a mixture of containers, including a large constructed wooden box (practically of raised bed size) at left center.

In many ways, rooftops are perfect for cacti enjoying a summer outdoors, as they love aridity and blazing sun.

Houseplants should be moved to the roof in the summer. Such dangers as insect predation, wind, and too much sun will be more than offset by heavy healthy new growth. Many tropicals need at least partial shade, however.

It is as difficult to plan an effective mixed planter before the flowers are full-sized and in bloom as it is to create that sort of garden on the ground, but it is easy to group containers to achieve the same effect. Containers allow you to take maximum advantage of the variety of blooming periods, sizes, growth habits, and colors of foliage and flower possible with annuals. You can arrange several containers on stepped shelves or group them in a larger planter filled with sphagnum moss, thereby having the intricate effects of a mixed flower bed without the abstract planning—and inevitable mistakes—such displays usually require.

One of the virtues of these summer flowers is that they can be taken casually. Bring young plants home from the nursery, set them out in suitable containers, and just let them grow. Most of them—certainly the ones listed here—are undemanding as long as they have root space and sunlight. Like vegetables, flowers are eager to grow. They provide lively bursts of color for the lowest expenditure of money and labor in the garden,

and give you encouragement and the time to care for the more demanding vegetables, bulbs, and woody plants.

If these flower lists seem skimpy, incidentally, it is not because few flowering plants can be grown in containers on the roof. In fact, many if not most can be, but the selection is so much a question of taste, sentiment, fashion, and availability that it seems wasteful to list the hundreds you might want to choose from. Read the seed catalogs, even if you want to buy later at the nursery, because they are one of the best sources of information on what flowers and varieties are available, what they look like, and what they require to thrive.

Use 5-10-5 or 15-30-15 soluble fertilizer on a half-strength, double-frequency basis, or mix a time-release form into the soil before filling the containers. In general, annuals should be picked if you want them to continue blooming. If you want the blooms to fade on the plant, just remove them before they go to seed.

Ageratum—Pretty mounds of (usually blue)

flowers which will bloom all summer long in full sun or light shade. Dwarfs are charming grown around the edge of a shrub container; the taller sorts make dramatic pot plants. Buy plants from a nursery for an early start, or allow about 90 days from seed.

Impatiens (balsam, *Balsamina*)—A large group of brightly colored, warmth-loving flowers that bloom all summer in shade or partial shade, at the base of shrubs or hanging from a basket. Impatiens is easy to grow from seed, but do not sow or set out young plants in cold soil as they may suffer a serious setback. Pinch to keep the plants compact and blooming.

Marigolds—This is an easy-to-grow, heat-and-sun-loving plant of deserved popularity. Nursery plants, or ones you start from seed indoors, should be set out in the warm soil where they will produce flowers all summer as long as you keep picking them. Marigolds come not only in virtually every shade of yellow, orange and red, but in many sizes, from 6 inches to 3 feet high, with flowers to scale. Many marigolds have a pronounced polleny fragrance which some people object to, but I find it delightful.

Morning glories, moonflowers, and cardinal climbers (Ipomoea)—There are gardeners who dislike these sweet potato relatives for their rampant growth but they are a joy on the roof. They are lovely in foliage and flower, grow energetically under adverse conditions and climb over and cover all sorts of eyesores. (A thick patch of morning glory can almost obscure a chain-link fence from late May through mid-September in New York.) Morning glories open early in the day, closing by afternoon, and come in shades of pinkish-red, white, and blue. Moonflowers open in the afternoon and are always (as far as I know) white, and cardinal climbers are, not surprisingly, red. All are beautiful, with heart-shaped leaves. The seeds are reputedly difficult to germinate (you can soak them overnight or scratch them with a file to increase germination) but I have never had any difficulty, even when I threw some out-of-date seeds onto the ground in a city park. They grew like wildflowers, and came back year after year, although the blossoms became smaller.

Nasturtiums—My mother used to call these "nasty urchins" because they always wandered out of their bed into some other, but we kids always loved them. They are cheerful, spicily fragrant, have edible leaves and sweet nectar complete with a spigot to suck it from. Aphids also love them, unfortunately, although you can usually control them with a daily hosing of the foliage. I prefer the relatively simple climbing nasturtiums, but there are other forms. Nasturtiums are always shades of red, orange, and gold. They transplant badly, but are easy to grow from seed sown in warm, dry soil.

Pansies—Pansies are perennials best grown (in containers, at least) as annuals, purchased as young plants from a nursery, but seeds are available, mostly by mail. Violas are similar to pansies, with usually smaller, striped flowers instead of the multicolored, "monkey-face" flowers typical of pansies. Both are delightful and perky looking grown around the base of a shrub. They need at least half a day of sunlight (preferably the morning). They are particular about having loose, cool, constantly moist soil, which makes pansies a little problematical on an unshaded roof, but you should be able to coax flowers during the late spring at least, if not all summer long. Keep picking the flowers to encourage continued blooming, though it will taper off despite all your efforts if there are several hot days in a row. Pansies, like strawberries, cannot tolerate having their crown buried. Be careful to plant them just as deeply as at the nursery.

Petunias—Voluptuous, bell-shaped petunias are easy to grow from seeds, but they also transplant well, and nurseries offer a fairly wide variety of types. Look for stocky seedlings and plant them in full sun or partial shade. Pinching will help induce bushiness at the beginning of the summer, and continued picking will encourage flowering as the season wears on. These are classic container plants, as certain to succeed as marigolds, and no garden should be without them.

Poppies (Papaver)—There are annual and perennial poppies; both are easy to grow and will flower the first year from seed sown in containers early in the spring while the soil is still cool. Move the container to full sun, but out of the wind, when the plants are established. Poppies should be sown every week or so if you want them to bloom over any length of time. Pick the flowers just as the drooping buds crack and begin to rise; cut the stems at an acute angle and dip them momentarily in near-boiling water, and you may get thirty hours out of the flowers. You will seldom get more, even on the plant, but it is worth every brilliant minute.

California poppy is not a true poppy. Among other differences, the California poppy can be induced to flower almost all summer long, and it has a nicer, carrot-like foliage than true poppies. These are as cheerful as real poppies, however, if not so large or spectacular. They are sturdy and adapt well to roof conditions. The traditional flower is single and some shade of orange but there are also multicolor and double mixtures available as seeds. California poppies may bloom from late spring through frost, and they are likely to pop up next year with the weeds, unless you discard your soil.

Portulaca (moss rose)—These easy-to-grow, spreading plants with flowers that resemble miniature roses (at least in the double forms) are heat resistant and are likely to grow and flower even if you neglect to water them. In the ground, many consider them weeds, but moss roses are charming when restrained to a rooftop container. Set transplants out after the danger of frost has passed (having germinated seeds indoors about 60 days before), or sow seeds directly in containers after the last frost date for late summer blooming.

Scarlet runner bean—Though a vegetable, this bean is usually grown primarily for its incredible red flowers and because it grows fast and hard in hot, sunny weather. The pods are tough when mature; keeping them picked encourages further flowering, but there are tastier varieties of beans for the table.

Snapdragon—Snaps are like hordes of deeply colored sweet peas growing along sturdy stalks, though there are also low-growing dwarf forms. The standards are very beautiful and relatively easy to grow, although you should begin with transplants, as germination can be difficult and slow. Like many annuals, snapdragons are sun lovers. Pick them regularly if you want to keep them flowering.

Sunflower—Sunflowers can be invasive pests in a yard but even though they are somewhat stunted in a container, they are wonderful flowers to grow on the roof. There is something triumphant about this tree of a flower—it rises above everything and would make an emphatic symbol for roof gardeners. The lower stalk is bare and not particularly attractive, but it makes an excellent support for morning glories, beans, or other climbers. Although there are dwarf forms, only meant to grow 3 feet or so, and fancy hybrids with double and multicolored flowers, I prefer traditional, yellow standard types, particularly *giganteus*, though it will only grow to 4 to 6 feet in most containers. The more soil you provide, the more height you will get, but a single sunflower can be grown (with three or four morning glories) in a 10-inch pot. Birds will come to eat the seeds; if you want them for yourself, cover the flower head with a cheesecloth hood as soon as the seeds begin to form.

Sweet peas—Sweet peas are old-fashioned, sweet-smelling flowers in shades of white, red, blue, and pink. The most useful are the vining forms, which are likely to give you the best choice of color and blossom size as well, but there are also dwarfs which, unlike the standards, do not need support. (They also make fewer flowers.) Although you can occasionally buy transplants, only take them if each plant is in an individual pot, as they do not transplant well. It is more common to sow seeds early in the spring while the weather is still relatively cool. As with edible peas, provide support as soon as you plant, as the tendrils form early. Sweet peas are heavy feeders, often grown in a deeply prepared trench in the ground, but they will make do with a quarter-strength, once-a-week soluble fertilizer program if you administer it reliably. Constant picking prolongs the blooming period, but long hot days may stop them no matter what you do; if your summers are especially hot, look for a heat-resistant hybrid.

Zinnias—Zinnias come in many sizes, forms, and colors—all the yellow/orange/red/pink shades plus white—and with flowers that resemble chrysanthemums, dahlias, or daisies. You can grow zinnias from seed (a good idea, as they have an aversion to transplanting) sown after the weather is warm. They love full sun, and keeping them slightly on the dry side (a cinch on the roof) will help prevent mildew, as will buying mildew-resistant varieties.

FLOWERING BULBS

Flowering bulbs (including corms, rhizomes, tubers, and tuberous roots) make excellent rooftop flowers, especially as many of them bloom early, when you are setting up your garden for the new season, or late, when everything else is fading. A bulb can hardly fail. The flower is completely formed when you buy it, patiently awaiting sympathetic conditions to expand and burst from the soil. If you plant it right at the proper season (usually the only time the bulbs are offered for sale) and at the proper depth, you are guaranteed at least one season's bloom as long as you don't drown it, let the dog chew it, or cut it in two while planting.

Planting bulbs in containers brings a special advantage; you can move the container to prominence for blooming, then out of the way while the leaves absorb energy from the sun before dying down naturally.

The most critical aspects of bulb culture are planting depth and soil drainage. Planting at the wrong depth will affect the height of the flower stalk but if you plant too deeply the flower may not emerge altogether. On the other hand, if you plant too near the surface, you may get too rapid division, resulting in smaller flowers (though more of them), necessitating frequent digging, dividing, and reburying. This is particularly likely with daffodils. Planting too near the surface also deprives the bulbs of the soil's insulating qualities, exposing them to drying sun or temperature ranges they cannot tolerate. On the other hand, planting too deeply is likely to prevent a healthy root system from forming. A simple (unfortunately, often unreliable) rule of thumb suggests planting two to three times as deep as the longest dimension of the bulb. It is a useful guide in a pinch but, frankly, I would rather rely on the advice of the bulb's supplier. Bulbs need space to spread their roots as much as any other type of plant. In general, while small ones (like crocus or grape hyacinth) can be grown in a planter 8 inches

deep, 12 or 15 inches would be a minimum for tulips, and 18 inches would begin to give them decent root space. A box 2 by 3 feet by 18 inches (or even 2 feet) will enable you to grow "a host of golden daffodils." Single large bulbs or clumps of small ones can be grown in an 8- or 10-inch clay pot. Although most bulbs are so amiable they will give you at least one good flower under almost any conditions, good deep soil may determine their continued success. It is virtually impossible to make a bulb planter too deep; any soil space not needed directly by the plant will help to insulate it from extremes of temperature.

Drainage is, if anything, even more important than planting depth. Bulbs are like onions (in fact, onions are bulbs); small bottom roots collect moisture and nutrients from the soil, but if the bulb itself rests in moisture it will decay, killing the embryonic flower within. On the other hand, because most bulbs produce heavy flowers on tall, slender stalks, they can use a slightly stiffer, more supportive soil than most roof plants, though it must still be well drained. The standard lightweight synthetic mixture will work but two parts of that mixed with one part of topsoil (that is, equal volumes of vermiculite or perlite, dark peat moss, and topsoil), with 2 to 3 teaspoons of bone meal per 2 gallons of the mixture worked in before planting is better.

When roof gardens were the province of the rich, it was common to use bulbs for a single season, then throw them away. Today, gardeners are more frugal, roof gardens are less formal, and bulbs are grown permanently in containers in which they spend their dormant cycle outside, just as they would in the ground. It is perhaps even better, because you have more control over their environment during dormancy. Nonhardy bulbs can still be grown in the old, throw-away way, of course.

Although each variety of bulb has a specific range of planting times, you should generally plant most spring-flowering bulbs sometime between Labor Day and Christmas and most summer-flowering bulbs during late winter or early spring, before the days are consistently warm. The autumn-flowering bulbs may in theory be planted in either spring or fall; usually, it is worth setting them out in late summer or early fall, when they are first available, as they may bloom that same season.

Soil in containers can easily freeze, thaw, and refreeze in the course of a winter, possibly heaving dormant bulbs from the soil. Consequently, bulbs—like deciduous trees and shrubs—need to be protected during dormancy. Planting in larger than necessary containers helps, as does placing inch-thick sheets of Styrofoam inside container walls before filling them, and using a deep mulch of almost any fluffy material. If you have a large unheated shed, containers of bulbs can be stored in there over the winter, or you can group them, stuffing crumpled newspaper in the spaces, covered with a tarp. The point is not to keep the bulbs warm, which could be disastrous, but to prevent temperatures in the container from changing so much that the soil alternately freezes and thaws.

The traditional bulbs—like tulips, daffodils, hyacinths, crocuses, iris, and grape hyacinths—are easy to find in local nurseries and garden centers but you may have to look for the more unusual bulbs in the catalogs of mail-order bulb specialists. No matter where you buy them, instructions on when and how to plant will accompany your order of any bulbs worth planting.

A few bulbs are listed here but if you feel experimental many others should be attempted. Bulb flowers tend to be more distinctive than their slender-rooted cousins so as you explore their varieties you may find many to loathe and to love, but only a few to feel neutral about.

Allium—This relative of the onion makes beautiful round flower clusters on a tall stalk, usually in shades of blue or violet. Plant bulbs as deeply as three times their height any time in the fall for spring flowers, or in early spring for flowers later in the summer. For drama, try a giant allium, which may pass 2 feet in height, in a 10-inch pot.

Anemone—Not every anemone is hardy but every garden can have at least some variety of this charming spring flower. There are traditional, single-flowering anemones in white, pink, and red as well as ruffled and double varieties in a wider range of shades. Plant them in full sun or light shade, 3 inches deep and 6 inches apart, in September for April flowers.

Crocuses—These wonderful, cupped flowers are really early bloomers. They come in creamy white and many colors; *C. speciosus* is violet with orange stamens, and there are others both more and less dramatic than that. Plant corms 3 inches deep, 3 to 4 inches apart in October, and have flowers in late winter (or at least by March). Autumn crocus will bloom this year if you plant them by the end of August. There are crocuses for most of the intervening months as well, which is part of their almost universal appeal.

Daffodils (and all other narcissi)—Gardeners plant daffodils in bunches and poets write about them for good reason—they are a moving sight in the spring. No one ever wrote kind words about the mangy leaves which persist after the flowers fade, however, as they slowly wither and die, which is why daffodils in a container can bring more pleasure than those in the ground. You can shove the planter out of the way somewhere as long as it receives at least four hours of sun a day. Plant the bulbs 4 to 8 inches deep (7 or 8 inches may be necessary to quell their strong impulse to divide and spread) in full sun in an 18-inch-deep container in August, and they will bloom in March or April. If it becomes necessary to divide daffodils (if the plants begin to produce more and smaller flowers), do it as soon as the leaves die and replant at once to give time for the plants to make good roots for the next year. If you are really cramped for space, there are also dwarf daffodils, which should be planted only 2 to 4 inches deep.

Hyacinths—Very fragrant in bloom, hyacinths are also extremely showy. For many gardeners hyacinths are the queen if not of all spring flowers then of the bulb flowers. They do not last so long as many other bulbs, and you may have to replace them after only two or three years. Set them 4 to 6 inches deep, one to an 8-inch pot or several in a neat row in a planter, preferably in September or October (but you can safely plant most varieties as late as December) for April blooming. Cut the flowers before seedpods form, to help lengthen their life.

Irises—Irises are my favorite bulb flowers, probably because they grew wild, mixed in a field with wild shooting stars, where I was raised in Alaska. Or it may simply be their beauty. The bearded varieties are popular in gardens but irises come in myriad forms and colors, from light blue and odd shades of yellow to a rusty orange-brown, not to mention all the purples and deep blues one thinks of in the first place. Plant rhizomes 3 to 6 inches deep in November; flowers will bloom in the spring or summer, depending on the variety. There are many growth habits and cycles among the many types of iris; follow the specific cultural instructions provided by your plant dealer. Remove the flowers after they bloom (if you did not cut them for your table) to prevent the formation of seedpods.

Muscari (grape hyacinths)—These are charming blue (or occasionally white) flowers on 4- to 6-inch stalks which appear more or less the same time as daffodils. Plant them in August or September, about 3 inches deep and 3 inches apart.

Tulips—Tulips are handsome, even arrogant looking. They provide a nice, austere appearance grown singly in deep pots, but the double-flowering, fringed, and streaky pastel tulips also look dramatic in groups. For the best selection, order early from tulip specialists (they won't ship the bulbs to you before they can be planted), and plant to the deep side of the recommended depths (probably from 5 to 10 inches) to discourage the bulbs from reproducing, which results in smaller and smaller flowers; tulips really look best when they are huge. Plant during late summer to early fall.

VEGETABLES

A desire for fresh flavor or freedom from pesticides in foods is often a motive for raising vegetables on the roof. Many city gardeners feel there is something almost magical about being able to produce one's own food, even if only in quantities better described as a garnish than a meal, as if one could become self-sufficient in the middle of the city. Many (if not most) vegetables are suitable for container growing. In fact, you can often succeed on your roof with vegetables that are difficult to grow in your region, as the roof is likely to warm up earlier and stay warm later than the soil just a few stories below.

No matter how many different vegetables can be grown on the roof, one is almost universal. Tomatoes seem to grow better in a rooftop container than in many gardens, and I have never seen a roof, fire escape, or terrace garden without at least one type. Lately, midget varieties grow tumbling out of window boxes or baskets hanging in southern windows as well. Cucumbers are fairly popular, as are eggplants, leaf lettuce and other greens with greater heat resistance. Corn grows phenomenally in roof heat and sunlight but produces such a small yield (two ears per plant, two plants of *midget* corn per five-gallon container) that most roof gardeners ignore it. Cantaloupes and squash do well but are also dramatically inefficient. If your goal is to lower food bills and increase nutrition by raising vegetables on the roof, efficiency will have to dominate your selection process. If you are more interested in the aesthetics of vegetables—in having a few wonderful tastes—it will seem quite reasonable to use four containers to raise eight ears of Silver Queen, or a whole trash can for one perfect pumpkin. Most of today's roof gardeners are interested in both the economy and the pleasure of raising fresh vegetables, however, so along with the high-yielding tomatoes and cucumbers may be a planter of early snow peas or cantaloupe.

Vegetables are almost entirely water. Success in growing them in containers is largely determined by your ability to supply it evenly and generously. Sometimes it is necessary to water daily during July and August, which makes a rooftop vegetable garden as much of a restraint on your social life as a dog is—you can't leave either alone for a weekend, for example. Rain is never an adequate source of water, incidentally. It is apt to weaken plants, in fact, by supplying trivial surface moisture on an erratic schedule.

Fertilizer is a related problem, as frequent and heavy watering washes many nutrients out of loose container soils. At the same time, most vegetables are using nutrients rapidly to support fruit production. Although it is possible to raise many vegetables in containers on pure compost or a mixture of compost and vermiculite—that is, if you have such a steady and voluminous supply of compost—you will have more control with a good

Vegetables, in wooden nail kegs, steel drums, shipping crates, cement blocks, and other "found" containers.

soluble fertilizer (one which includes both secondary and trace minerals in addition to nitrogen, phosphorus, and potassium), on a half-strength, double-frequency basis. Since nitrogen primarily feeds foliage development, it is better to use a formula which is lower in nitrogen than in phosphorus for the fruiting vegetables (tomatoes, peppers, and cucumbers, for example). Vegetables which are essentially foliage, like spinach or lettuce, can take more nitrogen, although I tend to use the same formula for all vegetables without ill effect, probably because the soil is so well drained that any minerals not used by the plants are simply washed through the soil. In fact, though it is dangerous to say this, it is difficult to overfertilize a plant growing in a loose, properly fast-draining soil if you always water until it drains out through the bottom and if you only fertilize after watering the plant.

Most vegetables need full sun for a minimum of six hours a day; most prefer eight hours, and if your skies tend to be overcast or smoggy, eight is a practical minimum. Roofs typically offer this much light but if yours does not, stick to root vegetables (carrots, radishes, and beets, for example) and greens (kale, lettuce, and some type of spinach), which have a good chance of doing well. Although midget vegetables are often recommended for container gardeners, standards—and

not even bush types—can help you use space more efficiently; you are limited in soil space, not vertical space, on most roofs. For example, staking tomatoes (indeterminates) will yield more pounds of fruit per cubic foot of soil and hour of care than bush types (determinates), and they can be tied to a trellis or stake to give them room to grow. Pole beans and peas also yield dramatically greater harvests than their bush counterparts.

Most vegetables and other annuals are heavy

Indeterminate (vining) tomatoes produce more fruits if they are tied to supports.

feeders. They shoot up from seed and produce fruit in two to four months; any setbacks—such as are likely with uneven watering or fertilizing or excessive heat or cold—may reduce yields or damage the flavor, texture, and appearance of the vegetables. Containers themselves retard growth somewhat, so your problem is to eliminate as many other potential barriers to swift, steady growth as possible.

Beans (Phaseolus)—Beans are not really a great roof vegetable, despite their love of hot sun, because they are so inefficient. A well-grown, pole plant may yield less than a pound of snap beans (and even less of shell beans), and you can grow only one or two in a cubic foot of soil. They have, however, lovely foliage and white flowers, and you may choose to take the beans as a delightful bonus. There are essentially two types of beans—limas, which you must shell and which demand steadily hot weather over a long growing season, and snap beans (which were always called string beans until the string was bred out of them), which you cook and eat pod and all and which come in green, yellow (or wax), and purple pods though the purple ones actually turn green when you cook them. Either type comes in pole or bush varieties.

Beans are actually beautiful vines, willing to climb almost any structure, as this photograph shows. They should be given plenty of root space, however.

Bush beans tend to be short-lived, so it is best to start new ones every couple of weeks through early August if you want them all season. Pole beans can be coaxed into producing until frost if you keep them picked. Bean seeds will rot if you sow in cold, wet soil, and they also respond badly to transplanting; unless you start them early in peat pellets or pots, it is best to wait until the weather is fully and reliably warm, perhaps as late as June, and sow seeds directly in your containers. It is best to use a legume inoculant with synthetic or pasteurized soils, as they will not naturally contain the beneficial bacteria which convert nitrogen from the air into soil deposits for use by the plant. It is inexpensive and easy to use. Plant seeds with the "eye" down and cover with moist fine peat moss no deeper than the diameter of a seed (even less indoors). Seeds germinate rapidly and some beans (but not limas) mature within 60 days.

Royalty, an early bush bean (55 days) with purple pods, is an excellent roof garden variety, as it (and most other bush types) will grow in a half-gallon of soil. *Cherokee Wax* is a yellow bush bean, and *Bush Romano* is a good, flat, Italian-style variety. Good pole beans include *Romano, Burpee Golden* (wax type), and *Crusader*, which produces 20-inch pods after striking red flowers. Prepare supports—at least 6 feet, preferably 8 feet tall—for pole beans before planting as they grow fast.

Beets (Beta vulgaris)—Beets are another vegetable you must not sow in a cold soil, though they prefer cool weather to grow in. They need 90 days to mature (although beets are lovely pulled at 60 or 70 days and cooked with their greens). You can grow a dozen beets in a cubic foot of soil, but they are likely to become woody and coarse if they are crowded, allowed to dry out, or run low on nutrients. *Burpee Golden* is tender and sweet but if you (like me) prefer red beets, *Ruby Queen* is good.

Swiss chard (Beta vulgaris cicla) is a sort of "beetless beet" grown for the greens, which to many people are tastier than spinach. There are essentially two types, one with red and one with white ribs, but they need identical culture and have nearly the same flavor. In most U.S. climates, chard will grow again in the spring if you cut its outer leaves back short and mulch it heavily over the winter.

Both beets and Swiss chard should be sowed (either inside early or in garden containers after the soil warms) about 1 to 3 inches apart, covering lightly with vermiculite. Thin to 4 inches apart, then pull every other plant for use as tender greens when they are about 6 to 8 inches tall.

Cabbage family (Brassica): broccoli, Brussels sprouts, cabbage, cauliflower, collards, kale, mustard—These vegetables are popular with traditional gardeners but few are truly suited to growing on the roof. Most cannot tolerate heat—they may bolt to seed or produce bad-tasting or tough vegetables—take too much space relative to their yield, or need an awkward growing season. On the other hand, Brussels sprouts are so absurdly charming looking that trying a plant (in two gallons of soil) may be worthwhile, particularly if you like Brussels sprouts. Cabbage is really difficult to grow well (it has many pests and ailments) and is so inexpensive to buy it is hardly worth any space (and it takes plenty) or trouble. Broccoli and cauliflower are also space takers, and cauliflower particularly needs special care.

Collards, kale, and mustard are a different story. Collards become huge (to 3 feet or more), even in a container if you are consistent in applying fertilizer, tolerate heat and cold (to at least 15°F.), and mature in 70 to 90 days, though they can be eaten at almost any time before that if necessary to thin the plants (or if you like young collards). Kale is somewhat smaller and somewhat faster to mature (30 to 60 days) and, well mulched and sheltered from the wind, will withstand not only frost (which improves the flavor) but snow. *Vates* is the classic variety, but *Dwarf Blue Curled* is also good and decorative as well. Mustard is often eaten 5 to 10 days after seeding indoors as a sprightly salad sprout, but cooked mature mustard is distinctive as well. *Tendergreen* most resembles spinach in flavor, while other varieties may strike some people as acrid or sharp. Collards are relatively inefficient, needing 2 or 3 cubic feet of soil per plant, but both mustard and kale will manage with six plants per cubic foot.

Except for mustard, the cabbage family can be sown while the soil is still cold; plant seeds an inch or two apart and thin after the plants emerge.

Carrots (Daucus carota sativa)—Carrots are a crazy kind of rooftop plant, but they taste so good

when fresh and young that they are well worth time and space. Begin early, in relatively cold soil. Soak the seed overnight, as it is slow to germinate, then sow 3 or 4 seeds per inch, and barely cover the seeds with vermiculite or fine peat. Thin twice, first to ¾ of an inch, then to 2 inches apart. Container must be a minimum of 8 inches deep, even for short varieties (a foot is better). A square foot will support perhaps 30 to 40 carrots. *Nantes* or *Touchon* have good flavor and mature within 70 days. Carrots will tolerate shade.

Corn (Zea mays saccharata)—Corn uses water and space wantonly. It is also decorative and delicious, and good corn is such a rarity in the city that roof gardeners should be tempted to grow it. Start seeds indoors (in peat pots or pellets, as corn dislikes being transplanted) or sow outdoors when fully warm (about 55°F.). *Golden Midget* produces 4- to 6-inch ears on a 3-foot plant, needs two to three gallons of soil, takes 60 days, and tastes pretty good. *Silver Queen* produces 8- to 9-inch ears on a 7-foot plant, needs four or five gallons of soil, takes nearly 90 days and is wonderful tasting. Corn must be no more than 2 feet apart to ensure pollination, and no other vegetable needs more water. Unfortunately, even on the roof you may get birds or corn worms which nestle in the husks and eat your corn while it is ripening. Covering the ears as they form by tying a paper bag over them may discourage the birds and dropping mineral oil in through the silks may prevent worms from hatching, but corn is one of the most attacked vegetables in the garden.

Cucumbers and *melons (Cucumis)*—Cucumbers and melons need space (12 gallons of soil for 3 plants) and a tall rack or fence to climb over, but young vine-ripened fruits are sweet and tender, and you can get at least five pounds of cucumbers or three melons from a single plant. All demand a steady supply of water and nutrients to thrive. Begin seeds in peat pots indoors and set the plants out when the weather warms.

There are many good varieties of cucumbers. Picked young, cucumbers are not supposed to be bitter, but *Sweet Slice* is supposed to stay sweet no matter how long it is on the vine. There are "burpless" varieties as well, bred for low acidity. My favorite is *Long Green* or one of the other Chinese-type cucumbers; you used to have to order them

Even cantaloupes (and midget watermelons) can be raised successfully in containers, if you have plenty of sun.

from Oriental specialty seed companies, but Thompson & Morgan is now offering three different varieties. There is also at least one midget, *Patio Pik,* but it is not enough of a bargain in terms of space and effort versus yield. Most cucumbers mature within 70 days, some as early as 50.

In melons be careful of the maturation period, as most watermelons and some cantaloupes need as many as 120 days. It is probably wise to look for disease resistance even when using totally synthetic soils as wilt can be spread by insects; it is discouraging to have the plant just wilt and die after it has set fruit. There are midget watermelons (*Yellow Baby,* for example) and cantaloupes, and they may be worth trying, as these plants are normally very expansive.

Eggplants (Solanum melongena)—Eggplants need more warmth and a longer season than tomatoes, though their needs are otherwise similar. They are handsome plants with large, spreading leaves and yellow-stamened, purple flowers, and the eggplants are dramatic as well as delicious. Start seeds indoors (or buy transplants) and set out when nights are 65°F. or more; two eggplants will grow in five or six gallons of soil and produce about ten fruits of one to two pounds each.

Lettuce (Lactuca sativa)—Head lettuces are too difficult to grow satisfactorily on most roofs, particularly in the summer, but there are many decorative and tasty leaf types that are well worth growing. No lettuce loves hot weather, and no lettuce likes to be deprived of moisture or nutrients. Sow seeds in cool soil with about ¼ inch of vermiculite over them; thin to 8 or 10 inches as lettuces grow (eating the thinnings, which are delectable on sandwiches). Crowding or any pause in growth will make lettuce bitter and nasty. It has relatively shallow roots so it can be grown in 6 inches of soil so long as the plants are far enough apart. Replace plants as you harvest them (with transplants or seed) to have lettuce throughout the season. Most leaf varieties mature in 40 to 50 days. There is a midget head lettuce, *Tom Thumb,* which resembles Brussels sprouts in size and is small enough to grow on a windowsill in winter, though the little lettuces are bizarre looking. *Salad Bowl* is one of the most heat-resistant leaf lettuces, recommended by one and all, but I find it unpleasant tasting, preferring instead to take my chances (growing early and late) with the red types or *Oak Leaf.*

Onions, Garlic, and Chives (Allium)—These are handsome plants yielding vegetables often more cheaply purchased than grown but worth growing in small volume nevertheless, if only in the form of chives for the kitchen. Onions require relatively

The most productive way to raise lettuce is to tuck it into odd corners, as these two plants have been.

Onions can be grown in containers as well, and their flowers are as decorative as those of many plants grown only for their blooms.

large amounts of water and nutrients, tolerate shade, and are slow to mature. They may be started from seeds, sets, or starter plants. I find it easiest to plant a flat of (about 100) sets as soon as ground soil is workable in the spring. The onions grow steadily, rising partly out of the soil, and can be pulled and eaten at almost any time. No matter how you start them you can grow three onions to maturity in a gallon of soil. If you want spring onions (scallions), start from seed or sets and use the young plants; a gallon of soil will hold about a dozen plants, and you can leave three to mature.

Garlic is also easy to grow. Plant five or six cloves (taken from heads of cooking garlic) 2 inches deep in a gallon of soil and water and fertilize until the leaves bend (usually 90 days) when they can be harvested. The green leaves are useful for cooking and salads, providing a gentle garlic flavor, but don't defoliate the plant or the bulbs may not form.

Chives from supermarket pots can be separated and successfully replanted, placing each 2-inch clump in a 6-inch pot. (They are usually root-bound and spindly when you buy them.) Clip chives regularly to prevent them from going to seed; you can freeze the excess for later use raw or cooked. Chives love full sun and regular (but not over) watering.

Peas (Pisum sativum)—Peas are really inefficient roof-garden crops (yielding 2 to 3 ounces of peas per standard size plant) but delicious fresh picked (even raw). They cannot tolerate hot weather, but you can start peas in cold soil early in the spring. Dwarfs, including some lovely Chinese "snow pea" varieties, need about a quart of soil per plant and about 6 inches of depth; standards need a half-gallon and a minimum of 8 inches. Be sure to supply a trellis or net for the peas to climb when you plant them as even the early shoots have tendrils and need support. Buy treated seed to protect against fungus (or buy Captan and do it yourself), and use legume inoculant if you are using sterile or lightweight soil. Avoid the extremely early, "far-north" varieties if you can and choose instead French-style tiny peas or such standards as *Early Marvel. Dwarf Sugar* can be picked young, when peas have just begun to form, and eaten Chinese style—pod and all. Begin to pick, from the bottom of the plant, as soon as pods have discernible peas in them; picking will encourage the plants to continue flowering but they will inevitably stop when daytime temperatures reach the 80s. Harvest most varieties about 60 days after planting seed.

These young peas are a second crop, to be harvested in the late fall. Note the tendrils already reaching up to the chicken-wire support.

Peppers (Capsicum frutescens)—Peppers are wonderful roof garden vegetables, as they are decorative and love direct sun. They are sensitive to temperature—if days are too hot and dry, blossoms may drop; if nights are too cool, blossoms may not form or may fail to set fruit. From the number one sees, many roof gardens obviously supply good pepper-growing conditions, however. My husband and I and our friends love spicy foods so we plant *Hungarian Wax* (mildly hot), *Long Red Cayenne* (hot for drying), green *Jalopeno* and *Fresno Chili* (hot for pickling and using in Mexican foods), but I also raise a dozen plants of Italian frying peppers (*Italianelle*), as they are at least as good in salads as bell peppers and are much better sauteed as they never get bitter. Set out plants as soon as the weather is steadily warm, allowing a gallon of soil *minimum* per plant.

Radishes (Raphanus sativus)—Radishes are usually recommended for children to grow or (because they are fast growing) to mark a row of carrots in a traditional garden, and that may be about all the plain red radishes are worth, especially as you can buy them so cheaply at the market. But there are more sophisticated and subtly flavored radishes, like the long, white, "icicle" radish and the red, black, or white Oriental types, that are well worth time and space to produce. Radishes grow fast and

Once these peppers started to grow, half of them had to be pulled to give the other three plants space, and they were still crowded. They produced remarkable yields, nevertheless, on this south-facing fire escape.

must be watered and fed regularly to prevent any check in growth, or they will be bitter and/or woody. Sow seed directly in cold soil, covered by about ¼ inch of vermiculite or fine peat, and thin to 2 or 3 inches as soon as they are up. Radishes may not develop if the weather turns too hot, and they will be happiest in a partially shaded place. Allow at least 3 inches more soil than the length of the long radishes and at least 6 inches for salad types. Harvest when ready—within a month for many varieties—as radishes tend to become woody and off-flavored when left too long in the soil.

Spinach (Spinacia oleracea)—True spinach is difficult to raise on the roof because it needs a long growing season yet is intolerant of heat; it also uses a lot of space relative to its yield. Most roof gardeners grow one of the other more suitable greens (Swiss chard, collards, kale, or mustard, for example) or grow New Zealand spinach *(Tetragonia expansa)* which withstands summer heat well, though it actually takes as much or more space than true spinach, and has an unspinach-like flavor. If you choose to grow New Zealand spinach (which is not a spinach at all), buy plants as the seed is difficult to germinate, and allow a gallon of soil per plant. All the spinaches like well-drained, moisture-retentive soils and regular feeding.

Squash and *pumpkins (Cucurbita)*—These gigantic plants are illsuited to raising on the roof because they demand not only large amounts of soil space (3 plants per 12-gallon tub) but vast climbing areas as well, though there are some midgets of pumpkin and bush summer and winter squash that are slightly more restrained. On the other hand, they respond so zestfully to full sun that it is worth having a barrel in a corner (especially if you want to cover an ugly stretch of wall) just to see them take off. Summer squash are the zucchini types, though not all are green; the skin can be cooked and eaten with the squash, and they can be sliced into salads if you lack cucumbers. The best of these is *Patty Pan*, as it seems to get less mushy when you steam it, but all summer squash taste a lot alike to me. Winter squash are basically the orange baking types which resemble pumpkins more than zucchini, although you can

Tomatoes and other vegetables will grow in 6- to 10-inch pots as well as in larger tubs, depending on the variety.

pick immature ones early in the season and find the resemblance to summer squash. *Butternut* or *Buttercup* are among the best. *Spaghetti Squash* is an amusing novelty (the interior of the squash looks like spaghetti) with a practical virtue—you can cook the squash intact, then cut it open to find the bland but crisp, pasta-like flesh which is more nutritious and less caloric than the real thing. Pumpkins are more or less just aggressive winter squash; the midget *Cinderella* is the most practical variety for the roof, and winter squashes can be substituted for pumpkins in almost every use except jack-o'lanterns.

All the squashes require, besides space, frequent feeding and a steady supply of water. They must have support to climb (or plenty of dry floor to wander across) as each vine is likely to take up 15 or 20 feet of space. Seeds will rot in cold soil, and the winter types and pumpkin need a long growing season (80 to 100 days), but squash are difficult to transplant both because of their roots and because they become huge so rapidly. Small plantable containers (the type used by growers for small trees, 4- to 6-inch size) or bottomless sections of milk cartons used as collars to hold peat will work; start no earlier than a month before the weather is warm enough to set them out.

Tomatoes (Lycopersicon esculentum)—Tomatoes are not the queen of vegetables for nothing. They are delicious and they grow enthusiastically, particularly in the typical roof-garden conditions of full sun, breezes, and plenty of water and nutrients (assuming, of course, that you are diligent about providing them). There are varieties for every taste and need, including low-acid types for ulcer patients and hybrids for short growing seasons, cool climates, and small containers.

There are essentially two types of tomatoes, vining (indeterminate) and bush (determinant) and several sizes of fruit, from 1-inch cherries to 4-inch beefsteaks. In general, your choice will come down to a nostalgic preference or an acceptance of what is available. I like tomatoes big enough to slice, of which *Big Boy Hybrid* is a good example, and Italian or plum tomatoes for cooking, of which *Roma* is typical. There are also several midget types: *Tiny Tim* or *Small Fry* (1-inch tomatoes) and *Pixie* (2–3-inch size).

Tomatoes will not grow if night temperatures fall below 56°F., and they must have seven hours of full sun to flower and set fruit. Buy transplants, or start seeds indoors in early spring, and set out after the weather is reliably warm. Allow from two to four gallons of soil per plant, growing three

Tomatoes and onions are compatible in planters, as both like moisture and full sun.

in a 12-gallon tub; the little cherry types can be grown in a 6- or 8-inch pot. Fertilize often but lightly to avoid excess nitrogen which will prevent fruiting, and you may need to shake the plants when they are in flower to ensure pollination, unless your roof is windy or attracts bees. I almost never prune suckers, because of laziness rather than ideology, but it is likely that removing them (the weak limbs which grow in the crotch where a bearing stem meets the central stalk) will induce heavier production overall.

KITCHEN HERBS

Many herbs are grown for fragrance, others more or less as ornaments; I grow herbs to freeze or dry for use in the kitchen. The roof is an excellent place for all kinds of herbs, as so many of them demand full sun, heat, and even relatively dry soil, and few of them grow larger than 2 feet. Although they vary by type, most kitchen herbs lose flavor if you overfertilize them, and most need frequent pinching to keep them in shape—a useful way to keep your kitchen supplied. While I only grow herbs that we like to cook with, there are probably two for every one in this list well worth experimentation. Although most herbs are

easiest to raise from transplants, many interesting types can be grown from seeds already in your pantry. I usually grow coriander (Chinese parsley) from kitchen seeds; if they have a low germination rate it is not low enough to pose a problem, and they are easier to find year-round (I grow it on the windowsill) than nursery seeds are.

Herbs seem not to be fussy about root space; if they are crowded most types freely adapt by growing less foliage, which is an advantage with the rampant types (such as all the mints). You can fit a basil plant in a tomato planter or an 8-inch pot, which will also support most others. Give the perennials more soil to protect them during dormancy, however. Growing different herbs together in a planter is often recommended, but I find that the pushy ones crowd the others out; it is easier to group several pots in a single box for the same look. The biennials can be most easily grown as annuals by setting out transplants from the nursery, but perennials are worth cutting back and mulching to hold for the following season; they need dividing every few years, however. Many herbs root easily from cuttings and can be grown in pots indoors, but I find them too demanding and have reconciled myself to dried or frozen herbs for winter cooking.

Basil (Ocimum basilicum)—This is a sturdy, spicy-tasting annual usually used with tomatoes and often grown in the same pot with them. It loves full sun but will tolerate some shade and should be sown, with tomatoes, either inside or in fully warm soil. The purple variety is said to be less flavorful and is usually grown as ornamental, but it is also good seasoning; sometimes a milder basil flavor is exactly right. Pinch flowers and growing tips to keep the plants bushy.

Caraway (Carum carvi)—Caraway is grown for its seeds, which you can certainly afford to buy at the store, but it is also a decorative, lacy-foliaged plant. It is biennial but hardy enough to start from seeds anywhere. It likes sun and well-drained soil.

Catnip (Nepeta cataria)—Catnip is an almost woody perennial castigated as a weed in some parts of the country. Aside from making your cat

happy, it makes a gentle tea. Catnip is a very hardy perennial, tolerates partial shade, and likes moist but well-drained soil. It is easiest to grow from transplants.

Coriander, Cilantro, or Chinese Parsley (Coriandrum sativum)—This is an annual, regularly picked at 6 inches for use as Chinese parsley, with a soapy taste you will either love or hate (for which use you should make fresh sowings every month or so), or allowed to grow to a foot or two when it will make seeds useful in Indian and Mexican cooking. It likes a loose light soil, full sun or partial shade, and should be grown from seed as its taproot makes transplanting difficult.

Dill (Anethum graveolens)—This is a huge lovely annual herb which needs full sun and plenty of fertilizer to thrive. Both the leaves (harvested at any time until flowering) and the seeds are used as

Herbs and houseplants not only thrive on the roof, they help make it lush while asking little effort from you.

seasoning for pickles or salads. (Catch the seeds in a paper bag whether you want them or not, or dill plants will turn up everywhere next year unless you throw out all your soil. Do not be fooled as I was into thinking this self-sowing tendency was a problem only in a yard garden.) Dill goes to seed fairly directly so you should make new sowings every month for a steady supply.

Mint (Mentha)—Mint likes moist soil, lots of nutrients, and light shade, but it will grow under diverse conditions. It comes in several varieties, all pleasant for tea or tossing with lightly buttered baby carrots, and all very pushy. Buy plants or root stem cuttings; cut the plants back and mulch for the dormant period, and they will be among the first plants in your garden next spring.

Oregano (Origanum vulgare)—Oregano is a very hardy perennial, a necessity for most Italian tomato sauces, and a lovely aromatic herb to have around. It demands full sun and exceptionally well-drained soil. Pinch the flowers out and replace the plants, rather than divide them, every few years.

Rosemary (Rosmarinus officinalis)—Although rosemary is a perennial it is usually grown as an annual from transplants. It is tolerant of soils and moisture conditions but likes strong sun. There are two forms—creeping and upright—but they seem to taste the same.

Tarragon (Artemisia dracunculus)—Tarragon is one of the most sophisticated herbs, prized by the French as a seasoning for light cider vinegar. It is a hardy perennial (to 10° below zero with protection), likes full sun or partial shade, warmth, and a mediocre soil. You must look for transplants of tarragon as the French form doesn't produce good seeds (it is propagated by division).

Thyme (Thymus vulgaris)—Thyme is a hardy perennial which also withstands dry soil, even drought, so long as you give it full sun. Pinch to keep the plant manageable.

FRUIT TREES AND SHRUBS

One hardly expects to find fruit trees or shrubs on a roof, yet several dwarf trees and small shrubs are well adapted for growing there. There are a few tricks, however. Even though mail-order

houses may offer a better selection, it is best to buy fruit plants locally, because they do not adjust very well to either warmer or colder climates. If the weather is too warm, the plant may not enter dormancy properly or emerge from it at all; if too cold, it may not live through the winter. Thus gardeners in the North may have difficulty finding a peach able to withstand temperatures much below zero, for example, and Southern gardeners may be restricted to a few apples or pears. On the other hand, one fruit or another will grow in virtually every garden.

It is possible to grow fruit trees and shrubs in lightweight synthetic soils, but they are usually better off in more supportive mixtures, such as equal parts of pasteurized topsoil, vermiculite, and dark peat moss (or compost). Most fruiting plants yield better when they do not receive too much nitrogen, but they should be fertilized regularly. Dilute solutions of 5-10-10 applied every week during the active growing season or a time-release form applied in early spring will do.

Even if you tend not to prune most trees and shrubs, fruit plants need some cutting back, particularly when young, to help them achieve an attractive and healthy form. Much of this shaping can be accomplished by pinching off new growth before it becomes woody. Later prunings may be needed to remove misdirected, damaged, or diseased limbs, expose interior branches to light, or remove nonbearing vertical branches, but you may also occasionally need to correct the form. Once you have done the early shapings and later remedial pruning, too little pruning is far better than too much. The assistance of an experienced friend or a good book (such as the Sunset *Pruning Handbook* or *The Pruning Manual* by Edwin Steffek) will be helpful. You will also need to thin the fruit as soon as it appears, at least for the first two or three harvests, to make sure the plant bears only as many fruits as can fill out and ripen. Failure to do this may prevent fruit from forming the following year.

Fruit plants are either hardy (capable of withstanding freezing weather to one degree or another) or nonhardy. Hardy varieties require the same sort of dormant care that other shrubs and trees need, but there is more at stake. If you lose all or part of one spring's growth because a fruit tree budded prematurely, you will get a reduced yield or possibly no fruit at all. (You can sometimes save a favorite tree that begins its spring growth too early by bringing it inside until the weather warms up. It should be hardened—gradually adjusted to roof conditions—before you return it to your garden, however.)

Although fruit plants have their own special pests, in addition to aphids which eat almost anything that grows, roof gardens seem to be relatively unbothered. Good housekeeping is the major defense, and applying an oil spray before buds open in the spring will also help by smothering any insect eggs capable of living through the winter.

Most dwarfs are produced by grafting, which means that the root system and the bearing top growth come from two different plants, although at least one popular tree—*Bonanza* peach—is genetically dwarfed. While grafted trees can throw suckers from the rootstock or, conceivably, even revert to the parent (root) plant (possibly taken from some other type of tree altogether), genetic dwarfs are the same, unalterable plant throughout. While some fruit plants are self-pollinating, most are not, and you must grow two—generally different varieties of the same fruit—within eight or ten feet to ensure good fruit production.

The surest dwarf for roof gardens is the *peach (Bonanza)*, but dwarf varieties of *apricots, nectarines,* and *plums* are also generally good candidates. All three of these fruits are energetic growers and require heavy pruning when young. Apricots are particularly likely to try to grow too early in the spring, necessitating protection until the weather catches up. There are probably more varieties of *apple* than any other tree fruit, most of which can be found as dwarfs as well as standards. Dwarf apples are among the most likely fruit plants to yield the first or second year after you set them out. They also should be pruned, mostly to shape them into a broad-based triangle so that lower fruits receive sunlight. Some apples produce little pollen; these types, which include *Greening, Gravenstein* and *Winesap,* must be grown with two other varieties to ensure fruit production from all three. *Pears* are similar to apples in form and growth habits, and most of the popular varieties can also be found as dwarfs. Pears also require at least two different varieties within ten feet for pollination. *Bartlett* and *Seckel* pears, two of the most popular varieties, are unfortunately unable to pollinate each other so if you want to grow these two you must also have a third variety. *Cherries* can be grown in containers but many so-called dwarfs top 10 or 15 feet in height, so beware. Cherries, sweet types particularly, are ambrosia to birds; you may have to cover them after fruits form if you want to have any for yourself.

Many other fruits are normally borne on small plants nicely scaled to roof gardens. *Bush cherries* come in varied forms, most of them small and decorative, and they produce fruit profusely, though it is probably better suited to cooking (that is, sweetening) than eating fresh. An old-fashioned favorite, the *elderberry,* should come back into style because the fruit, though tart, is distinctive and the plant is very handsome, particularly when it flowers in late spring. *Grapes* are good roof plants, although the selection of a type hardy in your area is crucial to success. Most grapes are easy to grow, but they do require specific kinds of care, particularly pruning, to thrive. Grapes must have support; they will climb all over an arbor, incidentally providing nice spots of shade during the summer. *Blueberries* are neat small shrubs, even if they don't fruit (and they won't unless you plant two varieties), but fresh blueberries are a treat. They need loose, moist, acid soil (use oak leaf compost or yellow sphagnum moss in the mixture), and possibly occasional supplementation with Miracid (as well as your usual fertilizer).

Strawberries are popular roof garden fruits. I have seen them growing in "pyramid gardens" of concentric metal rings (offered by many mail-order nurseries), but strawberry jars and plain tubs or boxes are more usual. Although the ever-bearing strawberries are supposed to lack good texture and flavor, I have enjoyed them (possibly because they taste wonderful compared to the Mexican or California berries which are picked green and shipped to the Northeast). They are fun to grow because they produce the first year, though you should really disbud the first set of blossoms to make later crops larger, and then make two or three crops each season until halted by frost. June-bearing strawberries, on the other hand, generally praised by strawberry connoisseurs for their flavor, give one crop a year beginning with the second year. Strawberries are sensitive about planting depth—they will not tolerate having their crowns buried—and must be kept moist and well drained, but otherwise they are easy to grow in full sun or partial shade. Be ruthless about removing plantlets when your container becomes crowded, as fruit will diminish if you don't. Sometimes the offsets produce few berries and should be discarded; if they flourish, however, pot them up in peat pellets and start another box or give them to a friend. Strawberry plants gradually produce smaller and smaller crops, after which (usually three to five years) they should be replaced.

WATER GARDENS

One usually thinks of water gardens as quiet places, full of exotic blooms and hints of perfume, found at the lowest part of marsh land or just around a point in the lake. To find waterlilies blooming sturdily on a roof is startling and refreshing. Artificial ponds, even if only in an old washtub, bring cool moisture to the hot roof and a very special group of plants into your life. You can grow water plants in a galvanized washtub, in a specially made pool, or in many other containers of appropriate size and proportion.

Water gardens are deep and mysterious; they seem to come out of our ancestral past. It is hard to imagine a person making one—they ought to be natural wonders, like rainbows or sunsets. Because of that feeling today's artificial ponds seem perhaps to be gimmicky, with built-in levels for every type of plant, predators for every pest, and chemically treated for every other condition. You can actually make a good simple pond fairly easily, however, and it will enable you to raise a few water plants on your roof.

A water garden is a whimsy on the roof. For weight reasons the pond must be small but because most water plants are perennials such a small tub may not hold enough water to prevent freezing, thawing, and refreezing capable of killing dormant plants. There is also an aesthetic

problem. Most water plants are large; if you try to grow much more than a single lily or lotus the tub begins to look ludicrously crowded. A small container is almost more likely to develop algae. These airborne, one-celled plants multiply rapidly in warm water in the presence of sunlight and are a natural and harmless occurrence in any body of water, however tiny. The condition called "green water" is simply water in which algae have become so numerous that it becomes green and murky. Well-established plants are an aid against algae, however. The large leaves of waterlilies block the light which algae need to grow, and underwater oxygen-producing plants inhibit algae growth by limiting available nutrients. In a small container, however, there may not be room for enough water plants to solve the algae problem completely, and there will be occasional unimportant surges in their growth. There are herbicides which work against algae but they are also potentially harmful to your lilies and grasses as well. Manual cleaning is probably the best way to keep algae under control.

Fish are inappropriate in a small artificial water garden. Many are cannibals in the first place but, even worse, they are likely to eat your young plants. If you have illusions of using fish to keep the pond clear of insects, you may be disappointed. Goldfish sometimes eat mosquito larvae but they are usually too carefree or lazy to do much real work. Finally, a small tub cannot supply enough oxygen or food (insects) to keep fish alive.

Each water plant must be grown in its individual container. This prevents rampant plants from crowding the less pushy ones out. It is also easier to place each specimen at its appropriate height if it is in a separate container, and the tub stays cleaner than when half filled with loose soil (though that is the best way to raise lotuses). The small planters should be of a type designed for underwater use, however, with holes in the sides to permit water to move in and out easily. Plastic is the more popular material today, and it is nearly indestructible underwater as well as inexpensive, but wooden boxes are traditional. Pots in classical, tapered shapes or of traditional clay or terra cotta are unsuitable.

Water plants will grow in almost any soil, although a mixture with a lot of clay (even 30 percent) is excellent for root support. Commercial topsoil is usually heavy enough. Do not attempt to use lightweight soil substitutes, as they will float to the surface, and do not use soils rich in organic materials, as they may continue to decompose underwater, producing gases which make the pond black, opaque, and sludgy. Excess fertilizer will have the same result, and it will be as available to the algae as to the more desirable plants. Water plants are able to derive most of the necessary nutrients and carbon dioxide from the soil and water around them.

To prevent soil loss when the container is first introduced to the water, line it with pierced plastic or untreated burlap and fill the container with soil to within a half-inch of the top. Place a flat stone or gravel on the surface near the plant. The lotus or water lily should rest with its roots (or tuber) covered by soil and the crown (or growing points) above the soil with stones or gravel on top. Keep the plants wet (in a bucket, preferably) at all times before planting, and place the container in the tub as soon as possible. Your dealer's advice on planting depth, fertilization, and ratio of plants to water volume should always be followed, since the immediate past history of a specimen will have a great deal to do with its needs for the future.

There are essentially five forms of water plants:

1. *Algae*—In a pond algae are pests. They are, however, harmless, natural, and, as individuals, fragile. Cold weather, lack of light (blocked by lily leaves, for example), or competition for nutrients and carbon dioxide (from underwater plants, for example) can kill algae overnight, and they also often destroy themselves by overpopulating. You can remove algae manually with a screen or cheesecloth net or, in desperation, use a chemical, remembering that it may harm other plants as well.

2. *Underwater oxygenating plants*—While not necessarily decorative the oxygenators help to control algae. Underwater plants should be placed, one cutting or bunch to a container, so there are at least ten inches of water above their soil. Begin with one or two plants for each square foot of water surface, and you will have to divide and remove some of them at the end of every season. A few useful oxygenators are listed below, and a visit to your supplier should reveal others.

Elodea (ditch moss, pondweed, water thyme, waterweed; sometimes labeled *Anacharis*)—One of the best underwater plants, with small fern-like leaves and inconspicuous flowers. There are several varieties, all useful and easy to grow.

Myriophyllum (water feather, water milfoil)—Beautiful plumed plant at least one variety of which (*M. proserpinacoides,* or water feather) produces its foliage above the surface of the water. (It also releases oxygen above the water.)

Vallisneria (eelgrass, tape grass, wild celery)—This is one of the most decorative oxygenating plants, with dark green foliage and tiny white flowers rising up above the surface of the water.

3. *Marginal or border plants*—Although in ponds these are divided into deep- and shallow-water varieties, marginals can be considered together as far as tub gardens go. (In describing any water plant as a "deep-water" variety, one is more likely to mean that the plant can endure deep water than that it needs it.) Marginals are traditionally found at the edges of ponds and lakes, waving above and often reflected by the surface. In a tub pond you may decide to grow only marginals, or to use a line of them almost traditionally with a water lily. This group includes the water grasses (sedges), cattails, and some flowering plants. Most will thrive with two or four inches of water over the soil. Marginals can be used alone, at the rate of one or two per square foot of water surface.

Cyperus (*C. alternifolius,* umbrella plant; *C. papyrus*)—These sedges grow below the soil while the stalks rise several feet out of the water. They are graceful, sturdy, and make delightful rustling noises in the wind. They will take winter outdoors in most climates, but are so charming and easy to grow that you might as well bring them in in a pail of water.

Iris pseudacorus (water iris)—This is a variety of the classical iris adapted to grow with about three inches of water over the soil. They are beautiful—so beautiful they can dominate a small pond; even waterlilies find it hard to compete.

Typha (cattail)—This group includes several varieties all of which are known as cattails. The varieties differ in height, the color of the cattail itself and of the stalk. Try to find a variety which will reach only four or five feet grown in a tub.

4. *Floating plants*—This is a group of plants with roots which need no support—they can literally be tossed into the tub where they will grow happily, probably even becoming rampant by the end of summer. Some floaters grow on the surface, helping to restrict excess sunlight and thus algae.

Hydrocharis (frog's-bit)—Decorative, tender, floating plants with large thick leaves and tiny white flowers on the surface of the water.

Lemna (duckweed)—Inconspicuous floating plants which form a gracefully patterned mass on the surface of the pond. They need to be thinned out periodically or they may clog it. The ivy-leafed variety *(L. trisculca)* is slower, more submerged, and less trouble, but harder to find.

Trapa bicornis or *natans* (water chestnut)—Hardy, edible, floating plant with leaves above and below the water surface. The fruit follows the uninteresting flower, and should be eaten when young. (If you enjoy eating the fresh water chestnuts so essential in Chinese cooking, this alone may be enough reason to have a water garden.)

5. *Lotuses, waterlilies*—These are the plants one thinks of as water plants. The broad leaves float on the water, surmounted by flowers with wide, spear-shaped petals, while the thick stems drift down, down into the depths. You are practically restricted to pygmy or miniature varieties in a tub and the "depths" are likely to be less than two feet, but the effect is still powerful. A small tub can support only one, perhaps two miniature waterlilies or a single lotus. Be guided by the people at your nursery as there are hybrids for almost any situation, in every color, blooming period, and size. There are basically two groups of waterlilies, hardy and tropical. You can choose among white and colors, some of which change during the blooming period; solid, variegated, or colored foliage; scented or unscented flowers; and day- or night-blooming varieties. The lotus *(Nelumbo)* is a related plant, very dramatic and easy to grow by itself in a twenty-inch tub, filled half with soil, half with water. All must have a minimum of five hours of full sun daily, and love to receive even more.

Once established, water gardens are nearly care-free. Few pests attack water plants (although some harmless insects may appear). There are enemies, of course, notably aphids which turn up in every garden, no matter how unusual or isolated. Other esoteric, more dramatic (and more destructive) pests—like bloodworms, diving beetles, leeches, and water boatmen—are rare except in lake country. Your supplier or county extension agent can advise you of special problem pests and tell you how to deal with them. Occasionally lily leaves are attacked by a fungus, although wind and the dryness usual on a roof help to prevent it. The most direct solution (and usually the only one required) is to remove and destroy leaves that have been attacked.

Mosquitoes do not attack water plants but they lay eggs on still water and use it as a launching pad to bother people and other animals. Mosquitoes can spread heartworm in dogs, and encephalitis, yellow fever, and malaria in people. Running a mosquito farm is a poor idea. A serious mosquito problem (which is unlikely to be yours alone, as they tend to become prevalent in a whole area) may mean you must drain your tub until the end of the breeding season.

Fountains, waterfalls, and spills—Moving water is delightful, particularly on the roof, but not in your lily pond. Most waterlilies and grasses barely tolerate movement, thriving in the calm places, not near a falls or in the rapids. But you can have a waterfall or fountain even though your garden is too dark or your roof too weak to support much of a pond.

Moving water is easy to arrange on a roof if you have access to electricity and at least periodic access to water and drains. The simplest way is to use a submersible recirculating pump and a tub, which can be of any shape and almost any size, but even more complex effects can also be contrived. A simple fountain where water rises from the center of a tub in a column and falls back down in a broader pattern around the source is possible with the simplest pump and installation. For variations, there are pumps which pulse or thrust the water up around a circle or other shape instead of through a single hole.

With a little more equipment you can make a

"wall" of water. The water is pumped from a long trough-like, ground-level pool to a slender open trough above from which it falls. This striking effect requires simple equipment, although mounting and leveling the upper trough may take professional assistance. Compared to the simple fountain this is special, and it is an excellent way to block out street noises.

The major problem with all water ponds, fountains, and other devices is weight. A cubic foot of water weighs 62 pounds. Therefore a trough 1 foot deep, 15 inches wide, and 6 feet long weighs 465 pounds, and you have the added weight of the containers and troughs. While many roofs can support that much dead weight, at least near the edge, it is doubtful they should be expected to bear much more, and the 7.5 square feet of surface water provided is really very small, visually speaking. Still, particularly if you live in a noisy neighborhood and need white noise (a gently distracting sound level), or if you just enjoy the sight and sound of moving water, a waterfall or fountain is worth trying.

Since I like things to look like what they are, I had a tiny fountain once in a washtub—up it went and down it came, with a lovely noise, and no secrets about it. That same simple fountain could have been made, however, to look like a weird but natural place with a material called Featherock, which is expanded lava, much like perlite, but in large sizes and colored and textured more like heavy stone. It can be sawed, drilled, glued, and moved easily, and it is uncannily rock-like.

6

Planting Time

The advantages of gardening on the roof show up most dramatically at planting time. You can do most of the awkward work—mixing soil, filling containers, and setting out transplants, for example—at standard table height, thus avoiding a spring backache. Rocks don't "grow" in containers as they seem to in the ground and, if you use sterile soil components, there are no winter-surviving weeds or insects to do battle with. Fragile seedlings which require shelter or shade can be properly placed, so you needn't improvise temporary protection. Of course, there are some drawbacks. You had to haul all those "convenient" soil ingredients and containers up to the roof in the first place, and roofs can be windy, uncomfortable places to work at any season. But at no other point in caring for your garden will you appreciate the convenience of your roof as much.

If there is any one useful rule for planting a roof garden, it is the old Scout motto, "Be Prepared." Although you can start a roof garden after succumbing to a flat of petunias in a garden shop, that is emphatically the wrong way to begin. First of all, you should already have a plan; even allowing for spur-of-the-moment purchases, take a list prepared from that plan when you go shopping. Secondly, realize that bringing home young shrubs or flats of transplants when you have no containers ready is like bringing home a new baby when you have no diapers or a crib. In fact, it is worse; babies are more adaptable (and more forgiving) than seedlings and young shrubs. Every-

thing you do at planting time should minimize the time plants are out of soil, particularly as most young plants are only sold when they are ready (sometimes more than ready) for planting out. Of course, practically speaking, plants can stay in a flat for a day or two, as can a balled and burlapped or container-grown shrub or tree, but no delay in planting is good. At best, it will do your plants little harm. Once you separate plants from a flat or unwrap a plant's roots, you must be ready to place those roots in soil. No plant likes to be stalled or shocked in the spring, but some—particularly annuals—may never have the time to recover.

PREPARING CONTAINERS FOR PLANTING

The containers you have bought, made, or found should have holes in or around the bottom for drainage, and spacers of some type beneath them for air circulation. If you plan to use wooden containers for shrubs or other long-term plantings, or if they are attached to the building or some other permanent structure, you should protect them against rot. One effective procedure is to waterproof by painting the interior and drainage holes with roofing cement or melted wax (heated in a can over boiling water to prevent possible explosions and fire), or by drenching (by soaking or brushing) the box with Cuprinol, which prevents or retards decay without making the wood nonporous. A quicker procedure is to staple or tack a trash bag or plastic dropcloth inside the containers, piercing the bottom to permit drainage. This has the further advantage of holding soil in without additional liners, but it cannot be considered a permanent solution, as stresses produced by changes in weather, plant watering, and root movement will make the plastic brittle and it will break eventually, probably within a year. It is probably safe to use found boxes for vegetables and annuals without treating them unless you want to oil or wax the nailheads to discourage rust (which needs not only moisture but oxygen to form).

Plastic, nonferrous metal, and ceramic containers need no protection from moisture but may need to have drainage holes added. Use furniture glides or casters for spacers, if you can attach them. These devices will not only provide air space but may help to make the filled container easier to move around (depending on the condition of your roof surface). All glides and casters should be of nylon or plastic and a nonrusting metal (such as brass or aluminum, but not chromed steel), or they will rust. Extremely large planters should have risers built in, or they can be set on blocks of wood, tiles, stones, bricks, open duckboards, or plastic lighting grids to raise them above the surface of the roof. Although this information was covered in depth in an earlier chapter and will be discussed again shortly, it bears almost endless repeating; in so many ways, the quality of the drainage will determine the quality of your plants.

If possible, soak empty containers of absorbent materials (wood, terra cotta) in water so they will not absorb moisture from the soil once they are filled. If the container is too large to soak, fill it with water after plugging the drain holes with corks, or add the soil, then keep saturating it until both the soil and the container can absorb no more. Allow them to drain overnight or until the mixture is loose, not soggy, and the outside of the box feels damp and cool, indicating an even level of moisture throughout soil and container.

Although you should be able to move any planter you use on your roof, most are heavy enough when filled—even with lightweight synthetic soils—that moving them is hard work, and rough on the roof surface. Try to place containers where you want them as early in the planting process as makes sense, given your working conditions.

Providing for Air Circulation

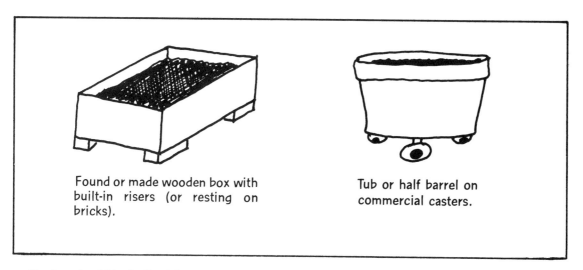

Found or made wooden box with built-in risers (or resting on bricks).

Tub or half barrel on commercial casters.

Planters should be built with risers as this wooden box is or set on bricks to ensure good drainage, cleanliness, and air circulation. Casters or furniture glides of nonrusting metal also serve to raise containers, making them easier to move at the same time.

Providing for Stability

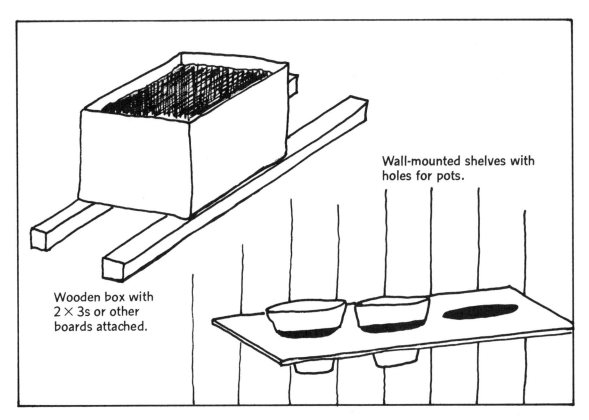

Wall-mounted shelves with holes for pots.

Wooden box with 2 × 3s or other boards attached.

Attached long runners increase stability for very windy roofs while raising the container. Shelves with holes sawed in them help plants in flowerpots remain upright despite rooftop winds.

STABILITY IN THE WIND

Regardless of which type of soil you use, tall plants in containers can be unstable on the roof—the foliage and any structure on which it is trained can behave like a sail in offering resistance to the wind. Minor instability can often be offset by moving a container from one position to another—from an uneven surface to a more level one, or from an especially windy to a calmer corner. A carefully located wind screen will also work on many roofs, as will using heavier or broader-based containers—although increasing the weight of a container merely to prevent tipping is wasteful and potentially damaging to the roof. It is better to build boxes with broad bases or with long runners on the bottom than to attempt to compensate for instability later, after planting.

Small containers can be blown over easily, unless you set them into holes sawed into shelves attached to walls or uprights for stability, or sink them up to their rims in vermiculite, peat moss, or expanded polystyrene (packaging material) in a larger, more stable urn, tub, or box. This system will also help to insulate small containers from drastic temperature changes; if the surrounding material is kept moist, it will conserve moisture as well, which is particularly useful for plants in terra cotta pots. Evaporation from the surrounding material will at the same time increase humidity around the plants.

Severe problems with stability may require attaching planters to the roof or parapet, either directly or by means of guy lines connected to the building and container by screw-in eyebolts. This is hardly an ideal solution, however, as the lines tend to be obtrusive—although you can train vines to cover them (and probably should to make them more visible, as the guy lines can be hazardous to people moving around on the roof).

PREPARING THE SOIL

Probably the most crucial requirement for plants growing in containers is good drainage. It enables roots to reach oxygen, water, and dissolved nutrients, while preventing dangerous accumulations of those nutrients in the soil. At the same time, however, the soil must hold moisture, to help offset the accelerated leaf transpiration and evaporation from soil and container walls especially likely on the roof. Since a completely natural soil is neither possible nor particularly desirable for most plants growing in containers, the simplest, most economical way to provide both good drainage and moisture retention is to use a synthetic soil containing equal proportions by volume of (1) vermiculite or perlite, which will loosen and lighten the mixture; and (2) humus (organic material), usually a type of peat moss, bark chips, sawdust, or compost, which will help the mixture retain moisture.

The soil will have different characteristics, depending on which specific ingredients have been used. Vermiculite and perlite are exceptionally light, and vermiculite actually absorbs moisture. Because they are so light, a small amount of either of these materials may float to the top of the container each time you water. This tendency seems to be greatest when the materials are used with sawdust or fine soil; the more fibrous materials (moss or compost, for example) seem to help hold it in place. Both vermiculite and perlite are functionally inert—that is, they have little effect on soil pH and provide virtually no nutrients.

While you choose a humus essentially for its ability to hold moisture, it may also affect the chemical and nutritive balance of the soil, depending on its level of biological activity. This effect seems to be negligible in containers supplemented frequently with dilute soluble fertilizers, but it is at least theoretically possible for humuses to alter the pH or nutrient level (particularly the nitrogen level) of your soil. Organic soils, of course, rely on this activity, but it could be a nuisance in synthetic mixtures.

Sawdust has a good consistency for containers but unless it is specially treated it can steal the nitrogen you have so methodically and expensively added to fuel its own decomposition. Even though the sawdust will later decompose (in organic soils, at least) and replace the element, it is foolish to gamble on it. Treated sawdust from nur-

Mixing Soil and Filling Containers

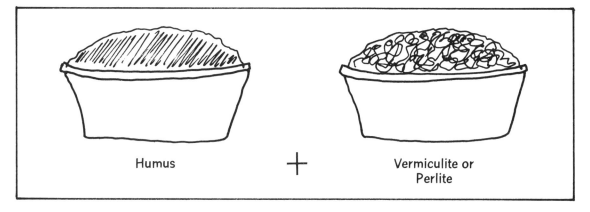

Equal volumes of finely milled peat moss and vermiculite or perlite make an excellent container soil for most types of plants. Sawdust, finely cut bark, or compost could replace the moss.

series, on the other hand, labeled "nitrogen-stabilized" or "nitrogen added," is functionally equivalent to the other humuses.

Some plants, notably blueberries, rhododendrons, heath and heather, prefer an acid soil. Although you can conceivably correct a neutral soil to acid by watering with dilute vinegar or by using products such as Miracid, it is far better to use an acidifying humus, such as light peat moss or oak leaf mold, to begin with.

Humuses also vary in their ability to hold moisture, with peat mosses clearly the most absorbent. They can hold an incredible amount of water though not when bone dry; the phenomenon is analogous to trying to pick up spilled water with a dry sponge—until it has absorbed some water and begun to swell, it is inefficient. Peat moss should be moist (that is, soaked, then drained) before mixing with other soil ingredients. The other humuses are slightly less absorbent and water-retentive than the mosses, but all can be used in container soils so long as they are suitable in other respects.

Compost has many virtues in the ground and, for organic soils, in containers as well. Its function is to decompose, however, and this process can be disrupted by the use of some synthetic fertilizers, so it may not work with synthetic soils. Furthermore, you must replace compost almost continuously as it disintegrates. Since many container plants develop shallow roots, working in compost (or any material) is dangerous. Other humuses also decompose but at much slower rates, particularly when used in synthetically fertilized mixtures. Using compost for mulch or in a column of chicken wire to nourish tomatoes, squash, and other vegetables works very well, even when the plants themselves are grown in synthetic soils, but it is homelier than you may enjoy in an ornamental garden.

Soils used for vegetables and other annuals should be replenished every year. At the end of the summer, consolidate the more or less clean soil from all the containers, avoiding obviously spent or badly contaminated material, and store it in a trash bag, leaving the containers clean and empty over the winter. In the spring, combine the old soil with an equal volume of fresh materials and refill your containers. Even on the roof, used soil may have collected weed seeds; use of a mulch will help keep them under control, as they can be just as destructive (perhaps more so) in a container as in the ground.

Mixing soils—It is important that soil components be evenly blended. This is especially true when you are incorporating bone meal, manure, or any other nutrient into the mixture. If your soil is unevenly blended, pockets of highly concentrated nutrients can burn a plant's roots and cause uneven growth. Roots can only grow and move in loose, moist soil, and thorough mixing is the only way to ensure that condition throughout your container.

The classic procedure for mixing large volumes of soil is to pile each ingredient on a separate dropcloth, shoveling alternate piles back and forth until everything is evenly mixed. Well, just try doing that, especially with materials like peat moss and vermiculite, on a windy roof! So much for that particular classical technique. I prefer to work in a plastic trash can. Flyaway materials are enclosed and the latched can is easy to roll and

These vegetables grow down through bottomless containers so their roots rest in a rich soil fed by the compost in the chicken-wire cylinder.

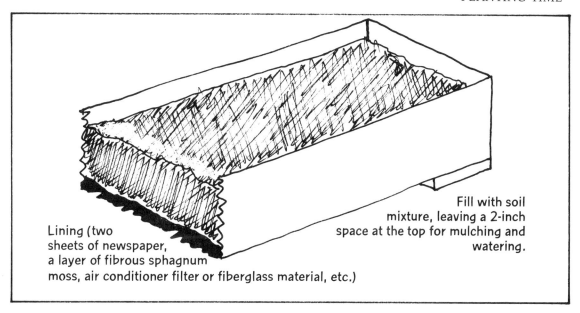

Lining (two sheets of newspaper, a layer of fibrous sphagnum moss, air conditioner filter or fiberglass material, etc.)

Fill with soil mixture, leaving a 2-inch space at the top for mulching and watering.

A separate drainage layer (of crocks, pebbles, or gravel) is not really necessary in a well-drained container.

jounce around until everything is well mixed. Fill only halfway, mix a few times with a large trowel or even with your hands (I use a long-handled Chinese cooking spatula), then close the can and roll it around, occasionally turning it end-to-end, until the soil is well mixed. (If you have children, they can often be drafted for this operation, which inspires great hilarity.) The can is also a good place to store the unused portion of the mixture until you need it again, as it will stay moist and clean.

FILLING THE CONTAINERS

The necessity to provide drainage holes in containers often conflicts with attempts to keep soil inside. You can resolve this problem in several ways. For a short-term container for annuals or vegetables you can line the bottom with two or three layers of newspaper, which will decompose within the season but will allow excellent drainage while intact and take virtually no depth. A slightly more durable lining is a layer of moist sphagnum moss or decomposable, loosely woven fabric, such as burlap or coarse cotton. For long-term planters—those used for shrubs, trees, or bulbs,

for example—a layer of screening of aluminum or fiberglass (but not galvanized steel) is excellent. Loosely woven synthetic (usually drapery) fabrics, such as polyester or fiberglass, work well, and so does air conditioner filter material. The classical solution is to cover each hole with a cupped section of broken terra cotta pot (or crock). This is usually combined with a drainage layer of more crocks, broken bricks, small stones, large pieces of perlite, pumice, or gravel. This system works well for houseplants in small pots indoors, but I almost never use it for vegetables and flowers grown outside in large containers, and I sometimes eliminate the drainage layer in shrub containers as well. A well-drained, moisture-retentive soil in a container with adequate drainage holes makes a layer of gravel unnecessary and using it just reduces the root space. Use of a drainage layer also makes reusing the medium in another container very difficult, as the gravel and crocks become mixed into the finer soil materials. At any rate, crocks tend to shift while you are filling the container, and soil is likely to be washed through the drainage holes when you water, despite your careful arrangement of crocks, unless—and this is recommended if you decide to use a drainage layer—you then cover that layer with newspaper, long-fibered sphagnum moss, burlap, or some other lining material as well.

Once you have prepared the bottom of your container, add loosely moist soil to the depth required for the plants, but no higher than two inches below the top, to leave room for mulching and watering. The container is now ready for planting much as a worked and raked garden bed would be.

STARTING FROM SEED

Although novice gardeners are often reluctant to start plants from seeds it is really not technically difficult, and it can be extremely rewarding. If you want to raise plants from another region or odd vegetables like spaghetti squash or yellow watermelons, raising them from seed may be the only way you can do it.

Seeds are meant to germinate. While each plant may prefer a specific environment for germination, most actually will sprout within an average range of conditions, which you can easily supply using simple homemade equipment. Several factors affect germination. The rate declines, first of all, with the age of the seed. However, most seeds dated for the current year will achieve at least 70 percent germination in the improvised germination boxes described here. (Germination rates under controlled conditions in a horticultural laboratory can approach 100 percent for fresh, high-quality seed.) Do buy this season's seeds, but if you happen to have some left over from last year, don't throw them away. Slightly increase the number of seeds you sow to compensate for their diminished viability. If you intend to use leftover seeds next year, on the other hand, wrap the packets of seeds in aluminum foil, crimped down tightly to exclude air, and store them in a corner of the refrigerator or other cool, dark place. It is probably inadvisable to freeze seeds, even though some can take it.

Seeds must also be old enough. This problem is only likely to arise when you collect seeds from your garden, and it is particularly likely for seeds of trees and other woody plants, which require

specific periods and conditions of dormancy. Purchased seeds, however, are always ready to plant.

There are also three strictly physical variables: moisture, warmth, and light. Moisture softens the coating and is absorbed by the seed, which enables the nutrients stored inside to dissolve and become available to the seedling. Too much moisture—wetness—causes seeds to rot. A lack of warmth may fail to trigger germination and growth. Most plants will sprout if daytime temperatures fall between 65° and 75°F. (dropping 8° to 10° lower at night). Certain vegetables—tomatoes and eggplant, for example—will germinate more successfully at 80°, though some proportion will germinate despite lower temperatures. If you know your temperatures are likely to be low, slightly increase the number of seeds per sowing to compensate for the reduced germination rate. Supplying heat from the bottom with heating strips designed for cold frames usually increases the germination rate but you are unlikely to need to do that unless the environment is quite cold—55°F. or less—or unless you expect the seeds to be unreliable.

You can assume that seeds will germinate in either dim light or darkness unless the packet warns that complete darkness is necessary. Bright light is never necessary until plants emerge. Seeds do not respond to light and, more seriously, light energy can heat enclosed germination chambers, turning them into steam cookers. As soon as true leaves (usually the second set) appear, however, the seedlings must have good light or they will elongate in search of it, and become spindly, floppy plants.

Starting Seeds Indoors

Gardeners often use the last weeks of winter to start plants indoors for planting later in the spring. This is the preferred way to grow tomatoes, peppers, and cantaloupes, which have a long growing season and cannot go outside until there is no danger of frost. There are many ways to germinate seeds on a small scale indoors, but the one described here is especially simple, because it is based on ordinary household materials. It works because it prevents three of the commonest causes of failure: (1) uncontrolled (too much or too little) moisture, (2) damping-off and other soil-borne diseases, and (3) transplant shock.

Even if you intend to use a natural soil in your garden, use vermiculite or fine dark peat, or a 50/50 mixture of both for germination. Not only do these materials provide an almost ideal balance of moisture retention and fast drainage, but they are also horticulturally sterile—free of the fungus spores, bacteria, weed seeds, and insect eggs often found in ordinary garden soils. Regular soils are also too heavy for fragile shoots to push through.

Use small individual containers to prevent transplant shock, which usually results when too many roots are torn in separating seedlings out of a flat, or when young roots are allowed to dry out before they are transplanted. Peat pellets are the most convenient form of container, but small pots filled with loose vermiculite, peat, or the combination are only slightly more work. Tiny plantable pots of pressed peat are more convenient than containers you cannot plant, but many ordinary household containers can be adapted. The tiny planters must be capable of supporting the medium long enough—say two to six weeks—to allow seeds to germinate and become hardened transplants. If the containers cannot simply be planted (as the pressed peat pots can), they must be easy to remove when the plant is ready for transplanting, which suggests the use of cardboard, paper, or thin plastic, and they must have drainage holes in the bottom, like all planters. Waxed paper, Styrofoam, or plastic drinking cups, frozen juice "cans," and plastic egg cartons, all easily punched for drainage with a skewer or other pointed tool, make good germinating containers, and your kitchen trash will probably yield many more. The important point is that each transplant must have its own, easily removed container to avoid entangling roots.

Moisten the medium before filling the containers. For relatively small amounts it is simplest to half fill a plastic bag with the material, then gradually work in water by kneading with your fingers through the plastic. When water begins to pool, the mixture has been saturated, and it should be carefully drained before using, until the medium is loose and moist, not soaking wet. Peat pellets must also be well drained, preferably not by squeezing, which makes the peat lump up, but by suspending them somehow (I use a colander or salad basket) for several hours or overnight.

Place the pots on drainage material in watertight trays and enclose them to regulate humidity. I used to use small trays—milk cartons or plastic juice jugs sliced in half the long way or frozen cake pans—enclosed in blown-up plastic bags, and that is still the easiest way to start a few seeds, but I have recently discovered clear plastic sweater boxes, complete with overlapping lid, which will hold several dozen small planters. Place drainage material, such as gravel, perlite, pumice, or fluorescent light diffusers, about half an inch deep in the bottom of the tray to permit a reservoir of water to collect without soaking the pots. To avoid confusion later, mark the trays now with plant identifications. The only markers I have found able to withstand the high humidity are indelible felt tip pens (particularly Sharpy brand) and grease pencils.

Plant two, three, or, at most, four seeds in each pot. If the seeds are too small to see and handle easily, place them in the fold of a piece of white paper and push them off one by one with the tip of a pencil or a toothpick. Overseeding is wasteful, as you will have to kill all but a single plant in each no matter how many start to grow there, and the crowded seedlings may weaken each other before you can thin them out. If your seeds are first-quality, packed for this season, which must by law be marked on the packet, you may get away with using just two, as virtually all seeds will germinate at a rate of 70 percent or better. If your seeds are old, if you had bad luck with that brand in the past, or you are experimenting with seeds collected from plants, use four to prevent wasting the container.

Place the seeds on the surface of the moist medium, cover them with a very thin layer of moistened vermiculite or moss taken from an expanded peat pellet. If you tend to be heavy-handed, it is much better not to cover the seeds at all than to cover them too deeply. A useful guide is to cover no deeper than the seed's diameter.

Enclose or cover the tray. Blow plastic bags up

slightly or prop up the lid so that it does not rest on the soil or the seedlings when they emerge. As you will need to open the chamber from time to time, don't seal it permanently.

The extent to which additional heat is needed will depend on what seeds you are trying to germinate and how warm your room is to begin with; most seeds will germinate faster or at a higher rate when some heat is applied, however. Small trays can be tucked into a warm place—such as near (not on) a radiator, behind or on top of your refrigerator (near the heat exhaust outlet), near your oven, on the back of a television set or stereo amplifier. Most seeds will germinate if daytime temperatures reach around 70°F., though 75° or 80° is even better (and necessary for some plants, notably eggplants and tomatoes). Preferably, the chamber should be several degrees cooler at night, just as it would be in nature.

By opening and closing the chamber, or misting gently with water, you can maintain a balance between too dry and too moist an atmosphere for emerging plants. The chamber should never become so humid that large drops of water form and fall down, or so arid that the surface of the medium feels dry to the touch. Changes in temperature affect humidity; so if you are not using a bottom heater, you should check the chambers in the mornings and evenings and at any other time temperature fluctuations are likely. Incidentally, I have found that most seeds will withstand slight dryness better than actually wet conditions, which cause them to rot.

As soon as the seedlings push through the soil, provide light. The best source is a fluorescent tube placed three inches above the top foliage of the seedlings. If you must make do with an incandescent reading light or sunlight on a windowsill, turn the tray daily to help compensate for light direction. If seedlings need to reach for good direct light at this stage, you are likely to end up with long-stemmed, floppy plants. When the first true leaves appear cut back all but the single strongest stalk in each pot. Be ruthless; if you wait for the strongest one to wear the others down, the process will have weakened it, perhaps irreparably.

Harden the plants to normal temperature and humidity by opening the covers gradually, for longer periods each day, and finally uncovering the chamber altogether. Unless the temperature is generally below 60°F. remove all heat as well, until the seedlings are accustomed to normal room conditions. However, if the room is heated by radiators, place pans of water or run a humidifier near the new plants, as such an atmosphere is uncomfortable even for well-established plants.

Begin to fertilize the seedlings as soon as you thin them. If you are extremely reliable, use soluble fertilizer at about ⅛ the recommended strength once a week; otherwise, use ¼ strength every couple of weeks. If you are using peat pellets or a commercial lightweight soil (such as Reddi-Mix or Terralite), which has had fertilizer added, use the dilute concentration of fertilizer every two weeks, unless the leaves start to turn yellow or the plants display some other sign of deficiency.

Because they are so small, individual planters of this type may dry out quickly, particularly as transplanting time approaches and the medium is full of roots. Water deeply whenever the top half-inch of medium feels dry to your probing finger, always continuing until water flows from the bottom of the pot, to flush nutrient salts out of the soil and to encourage strong, deep root formation. Transplant to the roof before the plants become rootbound or too tall to stand without external support. If the plants are ready before the weather is quite warm enough, move them outside under glass jars or other protection until the days are warmer. Even if the weather is mild, the transplants should be sheltered at first. While it is possible to transplant seedlings twice, once into a larger pot and then into large rooftop planters, it increases the loss due to transplant shock and doubles your labor.

Starting Seeds Outdoors

If you want to raise biennials or slow-growing annuals, you may have to start seeds indoors early in the spring or buy started plants from a nursery; but most herbaceous plants can easily be grown from seeds sown directly in containers. The only limitations are the length of your growing season relative to the plant's life cycle and the amount of container space you choose to tie up with seeds. Some vegetables and flowers are so difficult to transplant that sowing their seed directly is a horticultural necessity. You can raise two crops of short-season vegetables, such as lettuce, by sowing seed in the spaces left when (and as) you harvest the first crop, and you can sow the seeds of many plants outdoors before you can safely set them out as plants. About the only way to grow peas on the roof, for example, is to sow them in cold soil (they will even withstand light frosts) and harvest about the time you start to plant other vegetables. Eggplants and most varieties of beans, on the other hand, require warm soil to germinate. If the seed packet instructs you to sow "as soon as the soil can be worked" it means the seeds will sprout in relatively cold soil—in fact, it also often means that the plant is intolerant of heat—and you can sow directly in roof garden containers as soon as local ground soil has thawed. This kind of gardening enables you to get the jump on suburban neighbors, who must wait for ground soil to thaw and dry out before sowing.

On the other hand, if the packet recommends sowing only "in warm soil" you should obey, either by starting seed indoors or by waiting for warm weather outside, since without a heated greenhouse the seeds will undoubtedly fail. Not only might they not germinate in cold soil, those which do may be abnormal or stunted, fail to flower altogether or produce low yields, go to seed almost as soon as foliage appears or develop some other weakness—reasons enough not to waste your time or good seed by sowing too soon.

You can take advantage of the flexibility of containers when you germinate seeds outdoors before the weather is quite warm enough. Without building a greenhouse or even an electrically heated cold frame, you can often save a week or so merely by moving a container to the sunniest part of your roof, beginning a few days before you sow the seed, and leaving it there until the plants are strong and the weather is warm. Mulching with opaque plastic sheeting, tar paper, or other dark

material before sowing will increase the absorption of sunlight, thus warming the soil early. You will have to remove the mulch to sow the seeds, but you can replace it once seedlings are established, to help retain moisture and prevent weeds (yes, weeds, even on the roof). Once seeds are sowed, use a cover of clear glass or plastic, propped open to provide ventilation during the day, to form a mini-greenhouse.

If you are using a lightweight container soil, you can safely sow seeds directly in it. If you are using a soil-based medium, on the other hand, it is wise to replace the top two inches with these sterile materials, to prevent soil-borne diseases and pests from attacking seeds and seedlings, and to help you control moisture and humidity. When sowing directly in containers, sow the seeds slightly closer together than the packet recommends. Although this wastes a few seeds, as you will have to remove more seedlings, it will actually enable you to use container space more efficiently and give you more control over the density and arrangement of plants.

Once the shoots appear, thin by cutting the weakest-looking plants off at the soil line, leaving two plants for every one you intend to grow to maturity. After the second set of leaves appears, you can remove the extra plants in the same way, finally leaving only the strongest to mature. It is easier just to remove all but one as soon as the true leaves appear, but it is sometimes difficult to be so suddenly ruthless; this procedure gives you two chances to decide which seedlings stay and which must go. It also makes it easier to space the plants evenly in the container. Incidentally, it is always safer to cut the plants than to pull them out of the soil, no matter how loose it is or how undeveloped the plant's root system. If the roots of several seedlings are intertwined, which is almost unavoidable, pulling one can uproot another.

Once the weather is reliably warm and the plants are growing strongly, you can gradually harden them by removing caps, covers, and other protection. At this point, you should use a ⅛-strength soluble fertilizer once a week until the plants have several sets of true leaves, when you can begin to treat them like adult plants.

PROPAGATING BY OTHER METHODS

Division

Plants which grow and reproduce by means of bulbs, corms, rhizomes, runners, stolons, or tubers are among the easiest to propagate, requiring only that you separate or divide them. For convenience, I tend to refer to all these plants as "bulbs," although there are both easily visible and strictly technical differences among them.

Flowering bulbs—tulips, daffodils, and hyacinths (the most popular true bulbs), iris (a rhizome), begonias and dahlias (tubers or plants with swollen, tuberous roots which can be treated like tubers) and gladiolas (corms)—are often imported and are among the most expensive small plants at the nursery, but because they reproduce so easily many gardeners give bulbs away when lifting and dividing plants from an established bed. If you are patient, you can also buy a single plant and wait for it to produce offsets for division, assuming you want dozens of identical flowers—propagating by division always reproduces the parent exactly.

A plant must be divided when flowers increase or decrease in number and become small or pale, a sign that it is starting to choke on its offspring. You can also separate a plant before that point, sometimes as often as annually, but almost always after three years of growth. All bulb plants should be divided long enough after blooming to allow them to collect and store food for next season's growth (usually after the leaves turn brown and die), but early enough in the season to give them a chance to make roots and become established in the container before the soil freezes. I tend to divide bulbs as soon as the top growth dies, which can vary through the year, depending on when the plants bloomed.

Division is an easy, logical, and, in most cases, familiar process. You are actually dividing a bulb when you pull cloves of garlic from a head, a tuber when you cut a potato into eyed segments for planting, and stolons or runners when you remove a spider plant baby.

Like so many gardening processes, lifting, dividing, and replanting bulbs or dormant perennials can be more easily done than described. It is not a difficult or lengthy job. Since each individual bulb plant prefers a particular planting depth, refer to the label, catalog description, or the list in this book.

Most bulbs will grow in any well-drained medium with 1 to 1½ teaspoons of bone meal added to each gallon of soil. The container should be deep enough to plant the bulb at its recommended depth and leave a minimum of 4 inches for the roots. If you plan to leave hardy bulbs planted over winter, allow additional space for an insulating layer of soil, fiberglass, or a sheet of Styrofoam.

Traditionally, one lifts bulbs by sliding a trowel into the container and under the plant, removing the bulb complete with soil. If your container is small enough and doesn't have loose gravel or other drainage material in the bottom, it is easier just to turn it over onto a dropcloth or pile of newspapers. Gently shake and brush off bulbs, thus removing most of the soil attached to them, and set them aside. If you aren't working in the shade, cover the unearthed bulbs with a moist gunny sack or newspapers, as they must be kept from drying out. Lift only as many plants as you can replant in an hour or two.

The actual techniques of division are easy to master, as they are based on common sense. When they are mature, true bulbs, corms, rhizomes, and tubers contain a complete plant in embryo. When removing one of these from the parent plant, you must keep this embryo intact. This is easiest with bulbs and corms, which release readily when mature. Corms, which are less familiar, are divided by pulling the old corm off the plant and discarding it; the new ones can then be pulled apart easily. Tubers and rhizomes must be broken or, preferably, cut apart, using a sharp knife which has been cleaned in alcohol. True tubers, like white potatoes, have visible eyes; it is easy to divide them so that each section has at least two. Plants with tuberous roots, such as begonias, must be cut so that each section includes a dormant shoot or part of the central crown. Rhizomes, iris particularly, should be cut so each piece has a small fan of leaves (the leaves should be trimmed back to three or four inches first).

Many houseplants and herbaceous perennials which produce several stems from a central crown can also be divided—simply pull clumps of stems and roots gently away from the mass, discarding the original plant.

Cuttings

Propagating by cuttings is familiar to most of us. At its simplest, it is rooting a "slip" of grape ivy or philodendron in a glass of water, but the process can be applied to many varieties of plants, both herbaceous and woody. I will deal here only with stem cuttings, as they are most widely useful, but leaves and roots of certain plants will also take root and produce new plants.

Stem cuttings are of several types. *Softwood cuttings* (from herbaceous plants or from active new growth of woody plants) and *half-hardwood cuttings* (from mature growth of woody plants taken near the end of a period of active growth well before the onset of dormancy) are handled the same way. Choose a normal secondary branch (not the central stem), one that is healthy, has not bloomed, and which is neither exceptionally stout nor thin for the plant. Using a new razor blade or a sharp, clean knife, cut the stem about 5 or 6 inches back from the tip. Strip the leaves from the bottom 2 inches, or higher if necessary to expose two nodes, and insert the bare end in a relatively deep container of vermiculite, peat moss, or other sterile, moisture-retentive material. Mist or sprinkle the cuttings lightly from the top and enclose a tray of them in glass or plastic to form a mini-greenhouse or propagation chamber. (A blown-up plastic bag, a clear plastic storage box, a sheet of plastic film stretched across the top of a tall tray, or a glass jar inverted over each plant will work.) Set this chamber in moderate light (under fluorescent lights, preferably, but not in direct sun) until roots have formed—usually obvious when the plant perks up and begins to make new leaves—which may take 10 days or 6 weeks, depending on the plant. While most plants will take

root more rapidly in temperatures above 70°F., and many simply will not root below 55°F., the single most critical element in rooting cuttings—as in germinating seeds—is moisture. Watch the chamber carefully. There may be a mist inside the chamber, but actual drops of water condensing and falling on the plants is dangerous; reduce humidity by opening the cover for an hour or so. If mold forms, open the chamber and replace container and medium at once; there is a fair chance that the plant is lost, but quick action may save it. If the chamber becomes too dry, on the other hand, mist the plant lightly and reseal the chamber. Once the plant begins to make new leaves, you can harden them by opening the chamber daily for growing lengths of time, gradually normalizing its atmosphere, finally leaving it open. The plants are then ready to be transplanted into their own containers, although they should have protection from sun and wind for a few days.

Hardwood cuttings are taken from dormant woody plants after the leaves have fallen. Evergreen plants can also be propagated this way; wait until after the leaves have fallen from nearby deciduous plants. Rooting dormant hardwood is a slow process, taking several months or a year, and it is less certain to succeed than softwood cuttings. To offset this, one usually works with a bundle of branches to ensure success with at least a few. Roof gardeners are unlikely to have a handy source of shrubs from which to take cuttings, but the technique is useful as long as you can find a friend with a garden in the country. Choose strong branches, 1/4 to 3/4 inch in diameter, and cut them 9 to 15 inches long so that each cutting contains at least two nodes. Notch, tie, or otherwise mark the top of each cutting unless you are sure you can read the direction of the nodes. The traditional procedure is to band a bundle (perhaps 12 to 20 cuttings, tops together) and bury them horizontally in a box of moistened sand, vermiculite, peat (or a combination), until they form calluses and complete their dormancy. At spring planting time, each branch is placed vertically in a planter to root and grow. In a container garder, however, it is simpler to plant the cuttings vertically in the first place, deep enough to place a node at least 3 inches below the top of the soil. It may be necessary to cut back to within an inch of a node. While slightly more risky, this system permits the cutting to go through dormancy and enter spring growth without further disruption. Whichever approach you choose, the soil should be kept moist, but never wet, during dormancy as well as rooting and growth, and the dormant temperature must not rise above 50°F.—it is even better kept in the 35° to 40° range. Mulching will insulate somewhat and help maintain moisture but you should check the cuttings periodically during warm spells to make sure they are not budding prematurely, as the tender growth will die in a subsequent freeze, or if it is allowed to dry out. If your winters are too warm to maintain dormancy, wrap the bundles in moist sphagnum moss and plastic and store them in a refrigerator.

Layering

Layering is a gardener's version of "having one's cake and eating it too," because it enables you to root a stem while it remains on the plant; often, you can rejuvenate and salvage the parent plant as well, once the layer has taken and a new plant formed. It is the surest way to propagate many houseplants and garden plants with thick central stems or long flexible branches (such as Norfolk Island pines, dracaenas, and forsytnia).

There are several forms of layering. The most straightforward is "simple" layering. Wound a lower branch of a long-limbed, woody plant, such as forsythia, about 8 to 10 inches from the top. The wound should girdle the branch preferably, if it is thick enough not to break off and you can control the depth of your cut accurately; an alternative is to make a V-notch on the bottom (outward) side of the branch, wedging in a bit of toothpick to keep it open. Dust the wound with rooting hormone and bury the wounded section in the same or—more awkward but sometimes necessary—an adjacent container. Leave the growing tip and one or two sets of leaves above ground. If you plan to move the new plant once it is formed, sink a collar (an open-ended coffee can or cylinder of aluminum,

for example) first, then layer within its circle. The newly rooted plant will come out more easily with the cylindrical plug of soil. It may be necessary to stabilize the branch with a V-pin or staple made from a metal coat hanger. This method produces a single new plant from a branch. To produce several new plants from a single branch, try "trench" layering. Following the same procedures, bury a longer section, making wounds between pairs of nodes (but not between every pair).

A related process, "air" layering, works best on plants with strong, upright stems; it is frequently used on houseplants. Make a wound near the top of the stem just below the densest foliage and wrap the entire wounded area with moist, fibrous sphagnum moss. Cover the moss completely with plastic taped or tied around the branch both above and below the wound so that moisture cannot evaporate.

Most roof garden plants should be layered immediately after active growth ends and, even though roots may form earlier, should remain attached to the parent plant until the following season of active growth begins. They should then have protection during the subsequent winter, as they may not yet have a well-enough developed root system to withstand frost heaving or winter dehydration. Houseplants, of course, can be separated as soon as roots can be seen, as long as they continue to grow indoors.

To remove the newly formed plant, cut cleanly just behind the new roots. Place the new plant in a container at the same depth as it was buried while rooting and, if necessary, tie the new stem to a stake to encourage it to grow erect. Provide shelter from strong wind and sun for a few days, just as you would any transplant.

Rooting hormones—Synthetic compounds marketed under such brand names as Rootone—stimulate root formation. Plants which are difficult to propagate from cuttings or by layering will root more readily after an application of the material, which is usually applied in powder form. Plants that generally take root readily enough will do so faster. With most types of plants, the use of a rooting agent is optional, particularly when rooting a softwood cutting, but I would always use one when layering and rooting hardwood or when rooting any difficult plant (meaning one which failed to root for me before).

SETTING PLANTS OUT

Relocating is one of the five most traumatic experiences people undergo (in a class with death of a family member, major illness, bankruptcy, and divorce), according to a recent newspaper article. This relocation trauma is called transplant shock when it happens to plants, and it is the worst stress they can undergo.

Starting seeds or buying transplants in individual pots helps prevent transplant shock by enabling you to retain virtually all of a plant's roots and their surrounding soil. Hardening baby plants, by gradually reducing fertilizer, water, warmth, and humidity, also helps them get through transplanting by giving them time to become used to "short rations." Cutting back foliage and/or roots, especially of woody plants, may help them survive transplanting by reducing the size of the plant and thus its need for moisture and nutrients, though these steps are generally only required if there has been damage, to the roots particularly, before planting.

Virtually every plant needs protection for a few days—or even a week or two—after being set out on the roof. The shelter can be temporary and very simple, such as a folded newspaper tent or a collar cut from a paper towel core, usually sufficient to protect vegetables and flowers; a mini-greenhouse made by staking down plastic bags or inverting glass jars over the plants, sometimes needed when spring weather is unusually cool or you are trying to jump the season; or stapling a paper "cape" around a young tree's foliage to reduce transpiration by reducing the air movement around its leaves.

Transplanting into containers is essentially a simple project, which can be described in five statements: (1) Fill a container about halfway with moist soil or fill the container and dig a hole. (2) Rest the root ball (or bulb) in the bottom of the hole. (3) Add loose soil and gently firm it under and around the plant until it is supported and the hole is filled. (4) Water until water flows from the bottom of the container. (5) Protect the plant for several days, until it perks up and looks settled. (This is not necessary for bulbs.) The procedure is further refined to suit the needs of particular plants, of course, but this is really all there is to it.

Proper positioning within the container is important for healthy plants, though perhaps more for trees, shrubs, and bulbs than for most of the herbaceous nonbulbous plants. Bulbs have the most stringent rules regarding planting depth, as they are unable to bloom if there is too much or too little soil above them, but many trees and shrubs are likely to suffer various diseases if their old soil line is buried or if their roots are forced into a small container. Rose bushes, dwarf fruit trees, and other grafted plants should be planted with the bud union just above the soil line to discourage suckers from the undesirable rootstock. Strawberries and pansies are also finicky about planting depth; burying their crowns can be fatal.

Using an over-large container can cause compaction problems after a season or two (soil which has no roots extending through it can become waterlogged and airless). Crowding plants into an undersized container, on the other hand, is certain to be disastrous, even with lightweight synthetic soils. For one thing, extra soil helps to insulate against heat and cold, an important service on an exposed roof. For another, reserves of soil moisture help offset the drying effect of roof-level wind. Using an outsized container for trees, shrubs, and perennials may enable you to defer their next transplanting for a year or so or avoid it altogether—a good idea, since the older a plant is, the more traumatic transplanting becomes. Besides, trees and shrubs can become too large to transplant conveniently, even in containers on a roof. Finally, roof garden conditions (abundant sun, regular watering, and fertilizing) generally promote energetic growth and heavy root extension which a lack of soil space would inhibit. This dense root formation will enable a shrub or tree to go through dormancy in a container on an exposed roof and emerge with new growth in the spring, while less well-established plants may fail during their first winter.

Besides planting to the correct depth and in enough soil, it is important to set the plant into the container properly. Roots, when they are exposed, should be gently disentangled and spread so they can't grow into strangling knots. Do not leave absorbent materials—hardened clumps of soil, pieces of burlap, peat pellets or pots, for example—to protrude above the soil, as they may pull moisture out of the soil to evaporate in the air, or otherwise prevent its use by the plant. Never force a plant into a hole. The root ball, bare roots, bulb, or plantable pot should be placed on a flat-bottomed hole that is big enough to include not only the plant but your hand as well. Shovel soil in and firm it gently to ensure that it surrounds the plant. With few exceptions, set plants so their stalks are perfectly vertical, even if it takes two people and a carpenter's level to do it. Tomatoes, one of the exceptions, can be set sideways or extra deep so that only the top foliage is above the soil; the stem will right itself, and the buried section will provide supplemental roots and support. After planting, firm the soil, adding more as necessary, to reduce gradual settling later. Even though container soils should be moist to begin with, always water a newly set-out plant until the water drains from the bottom.

Leave at least two inches of space at the top of a container (one inch in flowerpots) and use it to mulch the plant. Winter (dormant) mulches should be fluffy and particularly well insulating (such as Styrofoam shipping pellets or loose straw); early spring mulches should be dark colored to absorb sunlight to warm the soil (black plastic or tar paper); and summer mulches should be moisture-retentive and decorative (chipped bark). Mulch immediately after transplanting to conserve moisture and soil warmth and to insulate against cold winds, using almost any material, including sheets of newspaper. Never apply mulch directly against the stems of woody plants.

Vegetables, herbs, and flowers are probably the easiest of all plants to set out. Few require any special consideration as long as their roots are neither damaged nor allowed to dry out.

Trees, shrubs, and woody vines are especially likely to suffer if you try to economize on the size of the container. Choose one big enough to hold at least two and a half root balls of the size you are planting and two root balls deep. While woody plants are generally offered for sale at a suitable age for transplanting, they are also likely to have been out of the soil for too long, particularly if you buy them from a city nursery, where the plants must be trucked in. The ideal would be for a plant to be dug, moved, and replanted within half a day. A plant is more likely to be out of the soil half a week or even half a month than merely half a day, if one counts the time it is on display at the nursery, travels, and waits for you to plant it. To minimize the trauma, have the planter ready—in position and partially filled with moist soil—before collecting the plant. If circumstances prevent you from being this well prepared—the planned container is too small or you have impulsively bought an unexpected shrub—it is better for the plant to wait a little, while you prepare an appropriate container than for its roots to be crowded.

A few hours before planting, water root balls thoroughly and soak roses or any other bare-root plants in a bucket of water. Fill the container about halfway with soil, beginning with a drainage layer if you intend to use one. It is helpful—especially for moisture-loving plants like the willows or any plant on a particularly windy roof—to improve the soil's moisture-holding ability by using a 2-inch thick layer of moistened fibrous sphagnum moss in the bottom of the container.

After watering once thoroughly, water again using a quarter-strength solution of 5-10-5 fertilizer, and then mulch (several sheets of newspaper, held down by stones, will work fine), being sure to leave a clear area of 1 or 2 inches around the stems to prevent disease and air problems. Shade the foliage with a paper cape, an umbrella, or some other temporary screen until the plant seems settled, usually in a few days. After you remove these wraps, watch the plant closely for a few weeks; if the foliage wilts, mist and shade it for a while.

Planting bulbs (and corms, rhizomes, and tubers, which are similar in culture) is not really so different from planting other popular garden plants, except for taking pains to plant to the right depth, which varies with both species and variety. Good drainage is the single most important factor in growing bulbs, but they also need a supportive soil to prevent the tall flower stalks from levering the bulbs right out of the container. A ratio of two parts synthetic soil (half vermiculite or perlite, half fine dark peat) to one part pasteurized topsoil will provide this stiffness and still drain nicely. Insert bulbs with the pointed end up, flatter side down, and be sure that the bottom and sides of the bulb are enclosed and in contact with the soil before burying them. The soil should be moist when you plant; water completely afterward until water drains from the container, and the bulbs will be off to a good start.

If you are planting hardy, spring-blooming bulbs in the fall, mulch the container heavily and place it under shelter with the dormant trees and shrubs, but you should remember to unwrap it as the blooming season approaches. Containers of bulbs planted in the spring or fall for fall blooming should, of course, be left uncovered until after they bloom, though they too should be mulched to keep the soil cool and to maintain moisture.

7

Maintaining the Roof Garden

It would be wonderful if roof gardens were maintenance-free but, like all gardens, they exact a price for the pleasure they give. They are easier to care for than traditional gardens, however, attracting fewer insects, diseases, and weeds. Plants, raised by containers, are at a more convenient height than they would be in ground-level beds.

ROUTINE CARE

Some aspects of caring for your garden are hardly work at all. Such important chores as removing insects and dead or damaged foliage can be done almost unconsciously as you harvest vegetables or pick flowers for your table. You can pinch the growing tips of the herbaceous plants, such as basil, coleus, and petunias, at the same time; it becomes an automatic response after a while. Other necessary tasks, however, are best scheduled and done on a regular basis. Watering and fertilizing are particularly important because you are using a fast-draining soil under typical roof conditions of heat and wind. Even though plants may survive if their soil dries out once in a while or if they run low on nutrients, symptoms of neglect such as wilting or temporarily ceasing to grow, weaken tissues and are harmful to the plants in the long run. If you fail to water or fertilize annuals regularly, they may not flower or set fruit; plants may drop their leaves, and any plant that has wilted even a few times seems particularly susceptible to insects and disease.

WATERING

Watering plants is a terrible bore, but it is a large part of the price you pay to have these amazing organisms on your roof. Almost all the special devices—perforated hose sections, canvas soakers, sprinklers—are nearly useless in roof gardens. A hose with a fine-spraying nozzle, however, capable of being turned off at the working end, is nearly indispensable. In addition, a good two- to five gallon watering can with a finely perforated head is excellent for watering seedlings and administering fertilizer solution. In a pinch you can even get by with only the watering can but it may curtail your gardening urges drastically, as it is certainly the hard way to water more than a few plants.

While I have never found that the hour plants are watered matters much, watering at the same time of day may help you to remember to do it and will help maintain even moisture levels in the soil. It is best not to water late in the day, when the air may be still and humid (which rarely happens on roofs) as fungus diseases could become entrenched. Plants vary—by heredity, size, age, and level of activity, position on the roof, and type of soil used—you should therefore usually not have to water every plant every day. Plants in small containers and most vegetables are more likely to need daily watering than slow-growing shrubs or bulbs which have already bloomed, for example. In general, plants should not be watered until the soil is dry two inches below the surface (one inch

106

in small pots, perhaps three or four in very large planters). The soil of dormant plants (including bulbs and their relatives) can be dry even lower before they must be watered, though they must not be allowed to dry out entirely. There are numerous exceptions to any rule of thumb for watering; overwatering is potentially more harmful than underwatering, but less likely because of fast-draining soil mixtures. Wilting (which can be caused, perversely, by either over- or underwatering) is a danger sign for any plant on the roof.

Always water slowly and steadily, covering the entire surface of the soil (since water moves almost entirely downward, not sideways), until water flows out from the bottom holes. This not only flushes undissolved nutrient salts from the container but moistens lower soil to encourage the formation of deep and spreading root systems. If plants are rootbound or the soil has been allowed to dry out, watering until you see water leave the container will not necessarily guarantee properly moistened soil, as the water will flow down the sides or through cracks to escape long before it is absorbed. In an emergency you may water such containers from the bottom (usually by immersion to the rim) until the surface of the soil becomes wet, but the real solution is never to allow a plant to outgrow its container—by pruning its roots or replanting—or soil to dry so completely that it shrinks and becomes hard.

FERTILIZING

Fertilize only after watering, and apply the solution until it drains from the bottom of the planter. In general use low concentrations of fertilizer (5-10-5, 5-10-10,10-10-10, up to about 15-15-15, for example) diluted to half or quarter strength but applied twice as often as recommended. Apply fertilizer on the same day of the week to give the plants a relatively steady supply and to help you keep track of your routine. For a few plants, mix the solution in a bucket and apply it with the watering can. Fertilizer solutions can also be applied with a sprayer; the concentrate in the sprayer jar is diluted as water flows through the hose.

Some relatively slow-growing plants, particu-

larly bulbs, trees, and shrubs, can be fertilized with dry powders or time-release pellets applied as directed on the package, as long as you watch your plants for signs of a deficiency. Mix the fertilizer into the soil or carefully scratch it into the soil surface. For plants with shallow roots, it is safer to cover the fertilizer with a thin layer of vermiculite. Always be alert to the possibility of a nutritional deficiency in container-grown plants, but many symptoms—yellowed or dropped leaves, a lag or slowing of growth, for example— could also be signs of over- or underwatering, over-fertilizing, disease, or pollution.

COMPOSTING

Compost is the material formed by the controlled decomposition of organic material. Suburban and country gardeners use the dropped leaves, straw, prunings (except heavy wood), many weeds, grass clippings, wastepaper, and household garbage (except meat and meat fat) to form a large compost heap, usually with three piles in varying stages of decomposition. This procedure is obviously impractical on a crowded and windy roof; furthermore, few roof gardens can generate enough material for large compost heaps. It is possible to make small amounts, however, by using a plastic trash can.

Aside from the organic material itself and the bacteria which consume it—normally present in sufficient numbers in the organic material used, but also available from garden centers as compost "starter"—both moisture and air are required to make compost. The length of time needed to convert fresh garbage to compost will vary depending on air temperature (warmer—faster), size of the particles (smaller—faster), and volume of the pile (larger—faster). Neither dry nor really wet material will decompose properly, and a lack of circulating air will also retard decomposition by killing some of the bacteria. Composting also occurs more rapidly in a mixture of materials than in just one or two (and the resultant compost is more likely to contain a useful variety of nutrients).

To use a trash can for composting, first make several half-inch holes in the lowest part of the bottom sides to allow accumulated water to drain. The trash can should also be propped up to facilitate drainage; three evenly spaced feet, purchased or made of scrap plastic or wood attached with brass screws will work well, but you can also simply prop it up on bricks. Leave a shallow pan under the can to collect the drainage, which is actually a useful starter solution for seedlings or a good mild supplement for a troubled plant.

The materials to be composted should be as nearly the same size as possible and the smaller the better. Putting kitchen waste through a blender is perfect but time-consuming, as the garden materials are likely to be much larger anyway. Do break stems and large leaves however, or they may decompose too slowly. The material should be moist as well. Kitchen garbage is often moist enough as it comes—particularly cantaloupe and watermelon rinds, lettuce scraps and bits of tomato—but eggshells, coffee grounds, dead leaves, and weeds should be followed by water. The excess will immediately run out of the can, particularly if you tip it around. For fast composting, the can should be about two-thirds full but it will of course start out with less. Each time you add material—and in any event once a week—toss the mixture with a small shovel to aerate it. You may want to clamp the can shut the rest of the time unless the mixture begins to smell bad; in that case, leave it open for several hours before and after turning the contents.

Composting does not always liberate noticeable heat. If there is no sign of active decomposition, however—heat, a reduction in mass, blackening of the material—within a week or so of filling the container it may be necessary to water or turn the mixture. Sometimes the addition of a source of nitrogen, such as bloodmeal or rotted manure, will also help to hasten decomposition. Commercial bacteria may also be added, though they are expensive and will die or be inactive if the conditions are wrong. In general, the material in the can will supply all the bacteria necessary for good composting.

Trash-can compost is limited in volume and, ordinarily, in the variety of its sources and thus its composition. It is the best humus for growing some plants, however, and it makes an excellent mulch. This method will reduce organic material to compost in two to four weeks during warm weather, and two trash cans could supply mulch, at least, for an average roof garden. Composting during the winter is slower but worth doing just to have the material at setting-out time in the spring.

COLD FRAMES

Cold frames sound useful but only after you have one will you realize just how versatile they are. You will wonder why you went for such a long time without one, as they can be used to grow lettuce and other greens during the winter, to germinate seeds, root layers and cuttings in the spring, to pamper a faltering plant any time, and to harden herbs and houseplants before bringing them in in the fall. In the country, gardeners assemble cold frames from discarded windows and doors. Few roof gardeners have access to those but a cold frame may be constructed of scrap wood, plywood, or metal or adapted from a shipping crate.

The box can be any size, as long as it is tall enough to root cuttings (at least a foot, allowing for soil and pots), small enough to reach all parts of from one, two, or three sides and to be covered with an openable, light-transmitting material—panes of glass or rigid acrylic plastic or heavy plastic sheeting, like that used to protect carpet runners. Interior temperatures during the day should normally be held between 65° and 75° F., sometimes going as high as 80° or 85° for germinating, heat-loving plants, with cooler ranges at night. These temperatures can sometimes be accomplished by sunlight alone, but you are likely to need a heat source for cloudy days and cool weather. Electric heating strips or cables are sold for this purpose (less than ten dollars in most sizes), and they are worth the money if you have a good outdoor electric outlet to use. Trays of vermiculite holding peat pots or pellets can safely be rested on the strips. No matter how you heat the box, or if you don't heat it artificially, a thermometer is essential, and you should check the temperature daily to keep the frame from overheating and killing its contents. Turning the heating unit off and opening and closing the top will help control build-ups of both heat and humidity.

Small cold frames are available commercially, many of them equipped like greenhouses with thermostats and automatic vents, but a simple homemade cold frame is useful enough for most roof gardens if you are around enough to keep tabs on it. Even a homemade cold frame can be equipped with a thermostat or timer if needed.

PRUNING

Although it is sometimes discussed as if it were an elective process, pruning or cutting back part of a plant is an essential part of good gardening. Normally one prunes away dead, damaged, or diseased branches, those which block the sun from lower parts of the plant or which press against another limb. You may need to prune a newly set-out shrub or tree to counterbalance damage done to the roots in transplanting. Pinching herbs or woody plants to make them bushy is a form of pruning, and it is preferable to cutting back later if you have a choice, as it is less traumatic. Young woody plants are pinched and pruned to encourage healthy branching and a good form, and it is maintained through annual light prunings. Branches bent by persistent wind or partially broken in a storm must be removed, as must old bearing stock on roses and some fruits. Shrubs and herbaceous plants can be trained to a standard (to grow with a single stem like a tree) through careful pruning, fruiting or flowering trees can be espaliered (trained to grow two-dimensionally against a wall) by tying and pruning, and shrubs can be pruned to topiary forms (to look like urns, chickens, or other objects).

To prune herbaceous plants or succulent growth on woody plants, pinching with your fingers or cutting with sterilized shears is sufficient. These methods leave clean wounds. If the branch is heavy and must be sawed, the project becomes more complex. To prune a heavy branch you first remove its outer portion; this will prevent it from tearing the whole limb from the tree while you are cutting, thus damaging the adjacent bark. Before sawing through a limb you girdle it (cut a slot

around the branch) to keep it from tearing bark from the plant as it comes off. Leaving a long stub (from where you prune to the next node or where that limb joins another) invites decay which may subsequently wander back into the tree; leaving virtually no stub, on the other hand, gives scar tissue no place to form so it also may involve other parts of the plant. Cut surfaces should be vertical so water cannot pool in them. If they are large or cavernous you should paint them with tree paint or melted paraffin (less permanent) to prevent insects or infections from entering the plant.

Some plants which bear flowers and fruit only on new growth must be pruned annually or biannually, in either the fall or the spring. Plants which produce winter buds must not be pruned late in the spring or they will not flower that summer. On the other hand, most spring-flowering shrubs should be pruned as soon as blossoms fall. Many shrubs and fruit trees may be pruned in the spring, after they leaf out, to enable light to penetrate.

While it is generally true that no pruning is better than too much, it is also preferable to remove soft green growth than to wait for it to become woody. It is also better to remove a failing limb before it breaks off spontaneously, possibly tearing bark or breaking another branch at the same time. Garden maintenance services do pruning, and it may be wise to have them do it for you at least once while you watch; it is bound to cost less than if you ruin established trees. Edwin Steffek's *The Pruning Manual* helped to take some of the mystery out of pruning for me, and the assistance of an experienced gardener, at least the first time you attempt to prune, is invaluable.

MULCHES

A mulch is simply a layer of material placed on the surface of the soil. Its use can help to conserve soil moisture, inhibit the growth of weeds, insulate the soil against extremes of temperature, supplement soil humus, or decorate the soil surface. Plants growing in fast-growing containers on windy roofs (and virtually all roofs are windy compared to the ground below) especially need mulches which increase moisture retention and insulate the soil. Virtually any mulch will do that, although fluffy types insulate better than flat ones. Any deep mulch will smother weeds and any organic mulch will eventually decompose and augment soil humus.

Mulches are needed year-round. In the early spring dark, light-absorbing mulches, like tar paper or dark-colored plastic, will help to warm the soil for early planting; later mulches will keep it warm until air temperatures become reliable. During the growing season, an inch or two of decorative bark chips or dark peat moss will help to keep the soil cool, deter many weeds, retard evaporation, and increase humidity at the soil line. Fall mulches will maintain soil moisture despite increasing winds and help a borderline plant live longer by insulating against fleeting early frosts. Deep fluffy mulches in the winter prevent alternating cycles of freezing and thawing which can uproot or kill dormant plants.

Traditionally, gardeners mulch with the most available material—hay, rotted manure, ground corncobs, leaves, grass clippings, seaweed, sawdust, pine needles, Christmas tree boughs— but mulches have also come to be victims of fashion—one year, fiberglass (like angel hair and equally hazardous to handle), the next year black plastic, then dried seaweed. In fact, if you simply use whatever you have or can afford, it will be incomparably better than using no mulch at all.

Certain materials are usually sold at garden centers and nurseries; depending on how many containers you have, buying one of these materials may be worth its cost. Peat moss makes a good summer mulch if you wet it before applying it, then keep it wet. The yellow or light brown mosses may acidify the soil as they decompose, however, making them more useful for yews, azaleas, or blueberries than for your other plants, but dark peats usually have no particular effect. Small stones or marble chips are decorative and useful on a windy roof as they help to hold other types of mulch in place, but they are heavy, tend to decrease insulation by compacting lower mulches and the top of the soil, and marble chips may release lime, thus altering the chemistry of your soil. Cut bark is my favorite mulch. It smells nice, is very beautiful, and both insulates and holds moisture well. It is also, unfortunately, expensive. Perlite in large, stone-sized pieces insulates well but it too can be expensive, and it is so light it is easily blown around. Sawdust makes a useful mulch but only in a nitrogen-treated form (available from nurseries) to prevent it from robbing your soil as it decomposes.

Many useful mulching materials turn up cheaply (if they are not free) even in cities. Since most places no longer permit leaves to be burned, you can sometimes get them from the collection service free or for a nominal sum. Recycling centers will turn your Christmas tree into small chips suitable for mulching, and many types of relatively clean trash can be shredded to use as a mulch. Shredded or cut-up Styrofoam (from coffee cups, meat trays, egg cartons, or packing material) is one of the best insulators, although you do need to cover it with something (a sheet of plastic, for example) to hold it in place. Black plastic is sold, rather expensively, at garden centers but dark green trash bags work about as well for a single season (the black plastic is heavier and made to be reused). In either case, the plastic can be used alone to blot out weeds and help the soil retain moisture, or it can hold an insulating mulch in place. Plastic can be tied around the container or to eyebolts set in the sides for that purpose, or you can weigh it down with bricks or stones. Newspaper is also an excellent mulch, though a homely one, particularly well suited to roof gardens because it is so available in most cities. It also needs to be held in place, however. Crumpled newspaper makes a pretty good insulator, useful between containers in the winter, and folded sheets of newspaper hold moisture next to the soil and prevent weeds from emerging during the growing season.

AS THE SEASON PROGRESSES

Remove short-season plants, such as lettuce, peas, or pansies, as they die, and either replace them with seeds or new transplants or empty their containers completely to foil weeds, insects, and other pests. Hose off filled containers every couple of weeks when you are watering the plants, being sure to direct the spray beneath them to knock off any pests that may have hidden there. No matter when a container becomes empty, scrub it (using a wire brush if the material can take it) and store it where it will stay clean. Examine and hose off beneath skids or duckboards as well, at least twice every summer, as insects like to lay eggs or hide underneath or between the boards. As long as you keep up with them, none of these chores become overwhelming, and many become automatic after a while.

As trees, shrubs, bulbs, and other perennial plants approach winter and dormancy, they need less water, fertilizer, and sunlight. The sun takes care of itself—days grow shorter and the sun's path becomes more oblique, but you must reduce the frequency of watering and fertilizing. Annuals and vegetables, on the other hand, will often produce until stopped by freezing weather—or frost, at least, in the case of tomatoes, eggplants and other warmth-loving types—and you can safely continue watering and fertilizing at normal levels, even though you cannot prevent the plants from reducing their production and finally stopping altogether.

Once the annuals are gone, and deciduous plants have lost their leaves, water all containers of dormant plants deeply and mulch lightly to retard wind-accelerated evaporation from the soil (using newspapers if no more decorative material can be found). After the soil freezes, add more mulch and protect against thawing by grouping the containers, insulating between them and around them with crumpled newspaper and covering the entire group with a tarp, or by placing them in a cold shed. Check dormant plants during the winter and water them if the soil feels dry several inches below the surface.

Remove dead plants and fallen leaves and turn out empty containers, saving the soil in a trash bag or can if it is clean enough to reuse. If you compost, dispose of leaves from naturally dead plants by adding them to the pile, or use them for mulching containers of dormant bulbs or shrubs, but plants that have died of disease should be removed altogether. Taking these steps will help prevent disease and insects from getting entrenched in your garden next year.

WEEDS AND INSECTS

The widespread persistence of pests, both weeds and insects, never ceases to astonish me. There seems to be no conceivable source, particularly in a roof garden, which is isolated from most other gardens and small enough that it would hardly seem worthwhile for the pests to make the trip. But they do. Even if you use synthetic soil and start all your plants from seed, so no insect or weed seed is brought into the garden, I guarantee you will see some of both once plants appear. Lamb's-quarters and lawn grass are the worst weeds, at least in my garden, but ailanthus sometimes pops its head through the soil, and so do various other plants on a random basis. The only reasonable remedy is to pull them the first time you see them and add extra mulch to inhibit the next batch. The first time weeds entered my roof garden I was amused by their temerity and lulled by their innocent appearance, so I decided to let them stay. "What harm could such little plants do," said I. Within a month of their arrival the lamb's-quarters had killed a sturdy marigold and a single blade of grass became a foot-long sheath. Take weeds seriously. On the other hand, don't go overboard; mulching and prompt hand-pulling will suffice. (Incidentally, young lamb's-quarters leaves spark up a salad nicely; it is obviously easy to grow, and worth keeping a pot of it just for that purpose.)

Insects are equally astounding, and much more maddening. Aphids appear almost the day lettuce pops through the soil and I spend the summer struggling against them. Aphids suck the juices from foliage, thus weakening but not usually killing the plant; they also introduce viruses which can kill unless you are raising resistant varieties. I must say that most of the vegetables and flowers they have so densely attacked in my garden survived; a climbing rose kept climbing and bloom-

Aphids appear as if by magic in gardens everywhere. They produce several generations per year, are able to survive the winter, and come in on many nursery plants despite your (and the nursery's) best precautions. Fortunately, they can be controlled by frequent blasts of water or water mixed with detergent.

ing despite aphids so thick they weighed the leaves down. Aside from being loathsome to see and think about, however, aphids can gradually weaken a plant and possibly kill it, and they should be controlled. Daily blasts of water from a hose or hand-misting with dilute soapsuds (1 teaspoon of liquid soap, such as dishwashing liquid, per 8 ounces of water) are usually effective. According to some writers (Cynthia Westcott and others), aphids and several types of moths become so confused by reflective aluminum foil used as a mulch around plants that they leave the plants alone, but despite a fascination with the idea I have never tested it.

Roof gardens also attract the standard houseplant pests. I don't know if they come along with plants raised indoors or are just so well entrenched in the city that the roof is a natural move, but they do inevitably appear. Their control is the same as it is indoors. That is, mist or hose plants infested with spider mites daily, being sure to go beneath the leaves where the little monsters live and construct their webs. Remove mealybugs and their egg masses (which practically carried a fuch-

Mealybugs are disgustingly quick to take over a plant. They can imperil a medium-sized fuchsia, for example, in a single week of neglect. These pictures show *(a)* an adult mealybug and *(b)* egg masses on a badly infested plant.

Juniper webworm is capable of involving an entire shrub or small tree in a couple of weeks. The catkin-like appendages *(a)* are cocoons formed of juniper foliage and a "paste" secreted by the insect. The close-up *(b)* shows one of the cocoons.

sia away last year during a one-week holiday; vicious bugs) with an alcohol-soaked cotton swab. Whiteflies attack tomatoes and fuchsias every single year, as well as many other plants on a seemingly hit-or-miss basis. I have never had much luck against these pests, though tomato dust slowed them down, but I understand you can use an oil spray in the winter to prevent their recurrence on woody plants, and that may reduce their general population. Scale attacks trees and shrubs as well as many houseplants, and it too responds to oil sprays applied when plants are dormant. You can also remove the scales with alcohol on a swab.

Woody plants in roof gardens are also attacked by their traditional predators. Besides scale and many varieties of aphids, which feast during periods of active growth since they favor young, succulent tissue, caterpillars which use a plant's foliage to spin cocoons often appear in late summer or early fall. Removing the caterpillars is the best control, and it is, of course, better to get them

before they make the cocoon than after. Vegetables attract a whole collection of unwholesome pests, most of which, fortunately, are sporadic or nonexistent on the roof (so far). Caterpillars, however—including tomato hornworms and cabbage loopers—can appear as they are the larval form of butterflies which fly everywhere. The easiest way to control these is by hand-picking (throw them into a jar of rubbing alcohol). Fortunately, Japanese beetles have not moved into roof gardens, as they eat every type of plant voraciously, are extremely hard to control, and are not above biting (or pinching) people. Because they go through the winter as grubs which feed on grass roots, however, they are unlikely to become too persistent in cities.

I only attempt to control bugs, not eradicate them. Fears about insecticide and innate laziness have brought me to this casual relationship with garden predators, which I loathe as much as anyone could, incidentally, but there are also practical considerations. For one thing, insects have never troubled me more than a friend of mine who grows the same sorts of plants I do and who uses pesticides, and all I had to do was squirt water selectively and pull a few nasties off the plants. Then, materials applied on a windy roof are likely to drift to some other roof or terrace or even to the streets below, for which I am reluctant to undertake responsibility. Finally, the few times I have used insecticides they didn't really work very well, and having been lulled into a false sense of security about their potency, I failed to take some generally useful measures and lost several plants.

8

Roof Gardens and Pollution

POLLUTION AGAINST PLANTS

Roof gardeners are often asked how they can garden in the city where there is so much pollution. Actually, although city gardens do grow in an environment different from their country and suburban counterparts, it may not be a more polluted one. Cities seem to produce more pollution than country places, but the trend seems to be to move factories, refineries, and other heavy industry out of the cities, into industrial parks or to rural areas where space and labor are cheaper. Furthermore, much pollution falls far from its source. A few years ago, when a huge skyscraper was being constructed in New York, researchers traced specially dyed asbestos particles (being blown into the building's walls as insulation) to see where and how far they went. The marked particles were found in several spots in the Northeast, some of them as far away as Boston, Massachusetts (two hundred miles away). Even if cities do produce most of the pollution there is no certainty that it stays there.

A pollution source may be fixed, such as an incinerator smokestack, or moving, such as exhaust from cars and buses. It may be particulate (dusts or pollen) or gaseous (smog or exhaust) or a combination. Not all pollutants are harmful to plants, and many plants are able to resist them—through native toughness, characteristic of weeds and a few other plants (like ginkgo and ailanthus trees), through careful hybridization in search of pollution-resistant plants, or through growth hab-

its which reduce the plant's exposure. Gardening in containers, on the roof in particular, also may help shield plants from some types of pollution. Because of these and other factors, city gardens may actually suffer no more from pollution than suburban tracts and country farms; on the other hand, it is a problem gardeners everywhere increasingly have to contend with.

The simplest way to handle local pollutants, such as a soot-belching chimney, restaurant vent, or dry cleaner's steam exhaust may be to block or deflect it from your garden with a narrow fence or screen placed a few feet from the source. If the discharge is illegal under local anti-pollution regulations, you can file a formal complaint, though results will be slow. Even if it is not illegal, however, regulations may require the polluter to vent the exhausts so many feet above any nearby building. This will not solve the pollution problem, of course, but such extensions throw the discharge into the wind stream, and away from your garden.

Diagnosing pollution damage is a tricky problem. Symptoms of disease, trauma, insect damage, or poor culture in general resemble the symptoms of pollution damage. By the time a plant is visibly damaged by pollution—since many of the symptoms are so generalized—it may also be under attack by insects or disease, as these agents often seek weakened hosts. This further complicates diagnosis. Some polluting agents cause distinctive damage—the metallic areas on leaves caused by growing in smog, for example. Unfortunately, it is necessary that contemporary gardeners be able to identify the effects of certain common pollutants on plants.

Peroxyacetyl nitrate (PAN) is the primary component of smog. It is a photochemical, produced by the reaction of nitrogen oxides with sunlight, and it is frequently found in combination with ozone. PAN damage may resemble ozone damage; it may also cause distinctive shiny metallic patches on the underside of leaves. PAN is not a serious problem in the Northeast, unlike ozone, which is troublesome coast to coast.

Sulfur dioxide is a common city pollutant, given off in the combustion of coal and petroleum-derived fuels, and it is especially serious wherever there is metal refining. Sulfur dioxide causes blotchy areas along margins or between the veins of leaves.

Fluorides are released by metal and ceramic processing plants. They cause the edges and tips of leaves (particularly young ones) to brown, dry out, and die; sometimes the damage is outlined by a thin, sharply drawn line.

Nitrogen dioxide is a waste product of incomplete combustion, such as gas leaking from stoves or in smoke, and it can stunt plants when present in low concentrations.

Carbon monoxide is also a product of incomplete combustion, and it is lethal to animals as well as harmful to plants, causing stunting and premature dropping of leaves and flowers.

Lead is given off by industrial processes and by automobiles using leaded fuel. It accumulates in the body and is poisonous to humans (and other animals), and it may be absorbed by plants, particularly leafy vegetables, then passed along to us when we eat them.

Ethylene is a component of old-fashioned household gas and some other fuels, and it is given off by ripening fruits and vegetables (in much smaller doses). Ethylene can cause blossom wilting, premature loss of leaves and buds, and tired, drooping new growth.

Salts is a combination term which includes elements essential (in tiny quantities) to plant growth, as well as others which are irrelevant or intrinsically harmful. Different salts are used to melt ice or prevent its formation on sidewalks and roads, to kill weeds, to fertilize plants and for

many other industrial and food-processing purposes. Some salts are also carried on winds from the sea. An excess of salts causes what we erroneously call fertilizer "burn," other types of scorch, and, if persistent or massive, death of the plant.

Since not all of the damage caused by pollution can be isolated from that caused by other agents, fighting pollution in the garden is mainly a process of good housekeeping or garden maintenance. A second approach is to choose plants with bred-in (or natural) resistance. Fortunately, many of the plant varieties especially well suited to growing in containers on the roof, or to city conditions in general, are also resistant to one or several forms of pollution.

Locating well-adapted, pollution-resistant plants is likely to be a process of trial and error. Normally, plants growing successfully next door, down the street, or even in a nearby park are likely to grow on your roof. City nurseries sometimes feature pollution-resistant plants, and new varieties are discovered every year. Often failures attributed to air pollution alone are actually caused by the gardener's attempt to grow a plant under grossly unsuitable conditions which, in addition to possible pollution, include such basically hostile conditions as intense sun and wind; frequently inadequate rainfall alternating with periods of storms; abnormal daily and seasonal cycles of temperature and light; and strange infestations of weeds, insects, and plant diseases otherwise known seemingly only hundreds of miles away.

Choosing pollution-resistant varieties of plants is not the only way to develop a resistant garden. Within any species varying growth patterns can make the difference between survival and death in the face of pollution. Because leaves are the site of transpiration and photosynthesis, a plant with fewer large leaves is more likely to sustain damage from pollution than a plant with a denser arrangement of small leaves; it has more leaves to survive and carry on and more foliage surface area to shield pollutants. Prostrate forms of plants seem to survive pollution better than tall-growing varieties, and sometimes one color does better than another, as white morning glories seem to thrive where the colored varieties grow but refuse to bloom. Polluted plants may drop old leaves a little sooner than normal but pollution can also cause young new leaves to drop.

In general, actively growing plants are more susceptible to damage than less active or dormant plants. Because rapidly growing plants require more water, nutrients, and light, they have a smaller margin of safety to protect them from assault. Similarly, a slow-growing plant is more likely to survive than a fast grower; since most pollution levels fluctuate daily or seasonally, a slow-growing plant will spend relatively more of its growing time under favorable (or at least unpolluted) conditions. Some vapors harm a plant by entering its metabolism; a more active growth rate permits the assimilation of more poison. For these reasons, you can counteract some kinds of damage by reducing water and fertilizer for a while, thus slowing the growth rate. In extreme cases, you can actually prune branches and roots, temporarily dwarfing the plant. Obviously, such dire measures are only justified when you need a little time to counter the pollution or move the plant—they are hardly the way to a healthy plant.

PLANTS AGAINST POLLUTION

Resistant plants can help to screen you from pollution, in limited though specific ways. Plants with textured or hairy leaf surfaces attract particles—which may include soot, seeds, or dust—by filtration from the air. All plants release moisture through transpiration, and it precipitates airborne particles onto the foliage. Whether filtered or precipitated onto the leaves, the particles are eventually washed to the ground by rain, where microscopic soil creatures metabolize them, returning nutrients to the soil. This will happen only rarely in the roof garden, as the majority of the particles will be washed to the roof surface outside the containers.

Plants can also mask or disguise bad odors. During the day, when their stomata are open, plants absorb and metabolize odorous vapors from the air, releasing oxygen in exchange. Consequently, you can place plants between an unacceptable odor source and the rest of your garden to help relieve the problem. If the plant itself has a strong but more agreeable fragrance, you will also replace the offensive odor with an acceptable one. Meanwhile, the dilution of the vapor-loaded air with oxygen produced by the plant is another way in which plants fight pollution, although the effect is slight insofar as a single garden is concerned.

Street lights and other city lights are not, strictly speaking, pollutants, but they are frequently an indirect cause of weakness and death in city plants. They encourage late growth and delay the normal onset of dormancy. Soft branches and new growth are begun too late in the season to harden off properly before the onset of cold weather, and thus succumb to the first hard frost. If your roof is at street-light level or below, this all-night illumination may pose a problem for your plants. Devices which block pollution, noise, or wind may help to shield your plants from city lights. Awnings, screens, or sheds may be placed strategically between street lights and your garden. Essentially, however, a roof bathed in light twenty-four hours a day has special problems, and you will at least have to avoid plants with extreme sensitivity to periods of light and dark.

In general, plants achieve their antipollution effects relative to volume. That is, in shielding your garden from pollution, more plants work better than fewer, tall ones work better than low ones, large leaves work better than small, and dense masses of plants work better than a few widely spaced specimens. But placement is also important. A single plant in the right place is more helpful than many elsewhere. A marked improvement in pollution control would require dense and widespread city greening, with plants actually replacing some people and buildings. However, what plants lack as physical antipollution devices, they make up for by providing visual and psychological relief.

Noise pollution is a special case. While it does not harm plants directly (as far as we know), it makes life in the city—and work in the city garden—increasingly difficult and painful. Noise has been indicted as a cause of high blood pressure and other stress-related physical illness, as well as numerous psychological disorders. It is more than mere irritating sound; it is uncontrolled energy attacking your body, and it is increasing everywhere, but particularly in the cities.

Sound is energy, like wind, running water, electricity, and sunlight. It travels in waves of varying pitch and length, with shorter waves having higher pitch. Each pitch has its specific pattern of movement (wave length), so that an anti-noise treatment is likely to be more effective against some wave lengths than others. This characteristic enables you to block some noises by tailoring the material and placement of barriers to the frequency of the sound. Sound is also relatively loud or soft, regardless of its pitch. This intensity is measured in decibels (db). Because the decibel scale is logarithmic, a 10 percent increase (or decrease) in decibels sounds like a doubling (or halving) of the sound. It is primarily the intensity of sound which damages eardrums, but people are also more sensitive to high-pitched than low-pitched sounds.

Sound waves travel from their source in a generally outward, fan-shaped pattern, with the path also influenced by wind and the climate. Energy is lost as sound travels through the air and when it is forced to change direction. It is finally "lost" (actually, changed to heat energy) when absorbed by a barrier. This loss of sound, regardless of cause, is called attenuation, and it is always described relative to a specific location. That is, noise which has been reduced to tolerable levels where you are may be blaringly loud just a few feet away.

The streets are the source of most general city noise, and distance is a good way to escape it, but moving to a tall enough building to escape noise is not always possible. There are specific weapons against noise, however. Since sound travels on the wind, hedges, individual plants, woven fences, or other devices used as open wind barriers also will reduce the intensity of sound. While the soft, flexible parts of the barrier absorb some of the energy, the firmer parts scatter or reflect much of the remainder. Your garden thus receives only a portion of the noise actually approaching the roof.

When sound waves encounter a barrier—which may be anything, including your eardrums—attenuation and redirection occur in several different ways, depending largely on the shape, composition, and location of the barrier. Smooth, relatively rigid surfaces, like a wall or a sheet of plywood, will send the energy away, toward its source (reflection) or in another direction (deflection). A faceted or otherwise regularly textured barrier will bounce sound away in many directions (scattering); and a deeply convoluted barrier can absorb sound, causing vibration in the barrier material and conversion to heat (absorption). There is a certain amount of attenuation when sound waves encounter any type of barrier, because some energy is absorbed or expended regardless of material. A barrier's ability to reduce sound depends on many factors other than its composition, placement, and design. Some of these are beyond our control, including not only the pitch and intensity of the sound, the distance and conditions between the barrier and the source, but also weather variables like humidity, temperature, rain or snow, wind direction and force.

Because sound waves spread as they travel, barriers are most effective at the source, where the energy is relatively compressed. Consequently, if noise in your garden can be traced to a single source, like a nearby ventilator fan or elevator motor, it will be relatively easy to block. Most city noise, however, is general. Tall buildings scatter and bounce sounds so the source of noise on any particular roof is actually everywhere. Protecting yourself from universal noise is difficult but not impossible. It is hopeless to try to reflect or deflect it. You would also not want to surround your garden with sound-reflecting material, even if such a project could solve your noise problems; such a solid wall would probably just turn your garden into an echo chamber. Absorption, on the other hand, is reasonable, especially where high-pitched sounds are the problem. Plants and other soft objects are effective sound absorbers. Awnings, shades, and plant supports of fabric or woven wood, plastic, reed, or bamboo (rather than metal) will help to absorb noise, as will soft floor coverings, like indoor/outdoor carpeting, rubber mats, or Astroturf. Plants are particularly effective in absorbing high-frequency sounds, like jet planes, fire engine and police sirens, or the screeching of automobile brakes. If you wanted an excuse to overplant, a roof with a lot of plants on it will have more protection from high-pitched noises than one that is less well stocked.

You can go too far, however. Complete sound blocking is impossible and probably undesirable. If you have ever walked through a Victorian maze of tall box or privet shrubs, you must have noticed the eerie, muffled, directionless quality of sound produced when virtually all sound waves are absorbed by dense, closely grown plants. Such complete sound absorption is uncomfortable for most people, so even if you could afford to surround your roof with ten-foot hedges, you would probably prefer not to.

Plants help in other ways to combat noise. Certain varieties of grasses and bamboo create a rustling "white" noise by moving in the wind. While it neither attenuates nor shifts unpleasant noises, the quiet sound of rustling leaves blurs the sharper sounds and distracts your attention. In fact, a garden has the overall psychological effect of distracting us from noise. While gardens do not always solve noise pollution, they do help us to live with it.

WIND

Wind is not really pollution. On the other hand, it is the avenue of noise as well as gaseous and particulate pollution.

Heavy wind is a poor condition for gardening. It can bend or break stems, whip leaves off branches, uproot young plants, or overturn lightweight containers. Steady wind can accelerate evaporation of moisture from the soil surface and container walls faster than you can replace it on a hot summer day, causing plants to wilt, fail to produce fruit, weaken, and even die. Such increased evaporation can be even more destructive during the winter when dormant plants cannot clearly indicate their need for water. Wind is particularly troublesome for roof gardens, because containers provide less soil and, consequently, smaller water reserves than a plant would have in the ground. Persistent low moisture levels or intermittent wet and dry periods can weaken a plant so badly that even a moderate wind is able to bend or break branches. Moisture loss can become

deadly in just a few hours on a hot, windy roof. Any steady wind, even a moderate one, can create problems in the garden. On some roofs, dealing with the wind is a major part of creating and maintaining a garden; on others, it is an occasional problem, or a problem on just one part of the roof. In fact, you will need to control wind on most roofs if you are going to raise a variety of healthy plants and enjoy doing it. The way to control the wind, however, is not always clear, primarily because of the way it behaves.

Wind is simply moving air. The movement occurs as different pressure zones form when layers within a mass of air are heated (by absorbing heat from the sun, for example) or cooled (by losing heat to a body of water), when they gain or lose moisture, or when they are compressed or released as they move over variations in terrain. Just as water flows downhill, air flows from regions of higher pressure to lower—the greater the difference in pressure, the stronger the wind. Wind is like water in many ways. Like water it can be absorbed and scattered; like water its warm layers rise and cool ones sink; like water it can swirl in to "fill up" a space; and like water it will flow until it reaches equilibrium, taking the easiest, most direct path to its normal level. Thinking of wind as if it were water helps to visualize its behavior in your garden. When a barrier—a plant or a fence, for example—is in the way of the wind, it must flow through, over, or around it to maintain its normal path, much as water must flow past a blockage in a stream. Passing through the barrier (past the leaves in a tree, or through slits in a fence, for example) causes less displacement and turbulence than passing over a solid wall. The wind actually loses some energy in passing through an open barrier by the friction of moving past the barrier material; the openings simultaneously absorb and deflect the air flow, resulting in a gentle, evenly distributed flow of air on the sheltered side of the hedge or grilled fence.

On the other hand, gusts of wind occur when air must force its way around or over a solid wall. Like water dividing to pass around a large stone in a stream, the flow swirls apart to pass, then together to intermix again as it resumes its downward movement, the air layers separating as they pass over the barrier and swirling together on the other side. The intensity of this swirling movement and the distance required for the flow to resume its normal path are dependent on wind velocity and on the shape of the barrier. The air changes in pressure when it moves over or around a solid barrier. When the lower layer of compressed, higher-pressure air emerges, it is forced down by the air layers above, and only its momentum prevents it from swirling down immediately to the ground on the other side of the wall. Actually, the swirl of air will occur several feet away, with the precise distance regulated by such factors as wind speed, height and shape of the barrier, and the distance between walls or barriers. It is this water-like pattern of air movement which

causes unpredictable gusts to attack your roof garden. The structures on the roof, or even on an adjacent roof, function as barriers to the wind, and your garden may be in the one spot where the wind must rage. Understanding how air moves, however, can help you control it.

Loosely woven fences of wood, bamboo, or metal mesh, with or without climbing vines or a row of plants in front of them, make good windbreaks for the garden. So do plants alone, at least under certain circumstances. A row of shrubs or small trees, for example, will break the wind's thrust, if the plants themselves are not harmed by the wind, and further if their containers are able to withstand its blasts. Usually, one ends up using some combination of fence and plantings.

Appendix

PUBLISHERS, PERIODICALS, AND OTHER SOURCES OF USEFUL INFORMATION

Energy Conservation with Nature's Growing Gifts, by William Flemer III, an offprint from the American Association of Nurserymen, available from Mr. Flemer, Princeton Nurseries, Box 191, Princeton, NJ 08540.

International Code of Nomenclature of Cultivated Plants—1969, American Horticultural Society, 2401 Calvert Street, N.W., Washington, D.C. 20008.

Arnoldia (formerly *The Arnold Arboretum Bulletin of Popular Information*); the title tells it all. One can subscribe to *Arnoldia* or obtain an index to past issues by writing to Arnold Arboretum, Jamaica Plain, MA.

The Avant Gardener culls and capsulizes technical and commercial horticultural news items from many sources. An obvious labor of love, valuable though erratically scheduled (probably *because* it is a labor of love), available for $10 for 24 (theoretically twice-monthly) issues, and well worth the money. Box 489, New York, NY 10028.

Trees Share . . . Unselfishly, free from Bartlett Tree Experts, 2770 Summer Street, Stamford, CT 06905.

Blair & Ketchum's Country Journal is a new, old-style rural publication, sophisticated graphically and in substance, with articles for farmers, gardeners, livestockers, and almost anyone with an interest in the country or the soil. $10 for eleven monthly issues (all except February) from the Country Journal Publishing Company, Inc., 139 Main Street, Brattleboro, VT 05301.

The Brooklyn Botanic Garden is one of the truly great sources of gardening information. Two publications, its *Newsletter* and *Plants & Gardens,* are included with a membership, $15 (and up) per year; copies of *Plants &*

Gardens are also sold through garden centers and nurseries. 1000 Washington Avenue, Brooklyn, NY 11225.

Building a Redwood Garden Shelter, Redwood Fences, Redwood Garden Structures You Can Build, and *Redwood Decks,* all from California Redwood Association, 617 Montgomery Street, San Francisco, CA 94111. Free ideas, working information, even plans.

Dover Books reissues many World War II and earlier home gardening books, texts (such as *Winter Botany*), and many other interesting books in paper covers at reasonable cost. Available from most bookstores or write to be placed on their mailing list, Dover Books, 180 Varick Street, New York, NY 10014.

Gardening with Saran Wrap offers suggestions for using plastic kitchen wrap as temporary mini-greenhouse material, some of them clever. From Dow Chemical Company, Inquiry Services, Midland, MI 48640.

Flower and Garden is a monthly magazine slanted primarily for suburban gardeners. Available for $4.75/year from Mid-America Publishing Corporation, 4251 Pennsylvania, Kansas City, MO 64111.

Journal of Forest History, quarterly publication of the Forest History Society, Box 1581, Santa Cruz, CA 95061.

Garden Way Publishing Company is a small publishing house specializing in organic growing techniques for gardeners, small farmers, cooks, etc. Current titles include *The Mulch Book, Greenhouse Gardening for Fun,* and *Growing Food and Flowers in Containers,* but new titles are added regularly. For list, write to the company, Charlotte, VT 05445.

Plant Growth Lighting, from General Electric Company, Lamp Business Division, Cleveland, OH 44112.

Sunbrella Outdoor Decorating Guide, free from Glen Raven Mills, Inc., Glen Raven, NC 27215. Suggested uses for fabric.

HHH Horticultural sells "almost every gardening title in print" by mail. Send for list/order form to 68 Brooktree Road, Hightstown, NJ 08520.

Horticulture is the beautiful monthly journal of the Massachusetts Horticultural Society, 300 Massachusetts Avenue, Boston, MA 02115. Available by subscription, $9/year, and well worth it.

House Beautiful's Gardening and Outdoor Living, an annual available on newsstands for $1.50 or by mail from 717 Fifth Avenue, New York, NY 10022 for $2. The 1975 edition included many features useful for roof gardeners.

House & Garden is a newsstand and subscription monthly which includes many gardening articles, a surprising number of them of relevance to roof gardeners. $10/year from Box 5202, Boulder, CO 80302.

Insect Control in the Home, Yard and Garden, Circular 900, University of Illinois College of Agriculture/ Cooperative Extension Service, Champaign/Urbana, IL.

Plants and Light, from International Light, Inc., Newburyport, MA 01950.

The Gardener's Almanac, by E. F. Steffek, published by the Massachusetts Horticultural Society, 300 Massachusetts Avenue, Boston, MA 02115.

The Mother Earth News offers a mixed bag of information, varying in reliability, sophistication, and orientation but all generally centering on self-sufficiency. Generally interesting if not specifically helpful. Six issues a year, available on newsstands for $2/issue or by subscription, $10/year, from Box 70, Hendersonville, NC 28739.

People, City & Trees; Man's Best Friend, the Tree; Trees Are . . . ; Trees—Helping to Clean Our Air???; Trees— Nature's Way to Diminish Noise; Trees Need Your Help, Too; Your Tree's Trouble May Be You!; and *A Tree Hurts, Too;* all from the Northeast Forest Experiment Station, 8616 Market Street, Upper Darby, PA 19082.

Shade Tree Evaluation Studies at the Ohio Agricultural Research and Development Center, by R. R. Chapin and P. C. Kozel, Ohio Agricultural Research and Development Center, Wooster, OH.

Home Vegetable Gardening, by J. D. Utzinger, W. M. Brooks and E. C. Wittmeyer, Cooperative Extension Service, Ohio State University, Wooster, OH.

Organic Gardening & Farming is a vigorous monthly, full of general and special interest articles emphasizing organic ways of growing. On newsstands (70¢) or by subscription from 33 East Minor Street, Emmaus, PA 18049 for $6.85/year.

Photosynthesis, a slender monthly newsletter of information mainly about growing houseplants but extending to container and other gardening techniques useful to roof gardeners, available by subscription from Photosynthesis Publications, 23 Sherman Street, Lynbrook, NY 11563, $6/year.

Plants Alive is a good-looking illustrated monthly magazine, primarily about houseplants but generally interesting. Available by the copy ($1) or by subscription ($9/year) from Plants Alive, 1255 Portland Place, Boulder, CO 80302.

Popular Gardening Indoors, a quarterly primarily on houseplants, which also includes articles on growing under lights, germination, and other general gardening subjects. Available on newsstands or from CBS Publications, Popular Magazine Group, 853 Madison Avenue, New York, NY 10017, for $5/year.

Starting Right with Seeds, from Rodale Press, Inc., Emmaus, PA 18049.

Julius Roehrs Company, Book Division, Box 125, East Rutherford, NJ 07073, is the publisher of such basic reference books on houseplants as *Exotica, Exotic Plant Manual,* as well as other occasional books.

Do It Yourself with Plexiglas gives instructions for using (forming, polishing, sawing, etc.) acrylic sheet plastics, from Rohm & Haas, Philadelphia, PA 19105.

How to Prune and Trim, 25¢ from Seymour Smith & Son, Inc., Oakville, CT 06779, manufacturers of Snapcut pruning tools.

The Good Earth Can Do Your Dirt! and *The Organic Supplement* (50¢), from Sudbury Laboratory, Inc., Sudbury, MA 01776.

Sunset, the Magazine of Western Living publishes many articles on gardening and on garden facilities. Available on newsstands in Western cities or by subscription from Sunset Magazine, Menlo Park, CA 94025, $6/year to the nine Western states, $9/year elsewhere in the U.S.

Brief History of Measurement Systems, from the National Bureau of Standards, available from the Superintendent of Documents, U.S. Government Printing Office, Washington, D.C. 20402.

Shrubs, Vines and Trees for Summer Color, Growing Vegetables in the Home Garden, Growing Plants without Soil for Experimental Use —a few of the many U.S.D.A. bulletins also available at small cost from the Superintendent of Documents.

Trees and Shrubs for Noise Abatement, an excellent sourcebook by D. I. Cook and D. F. Van Haverbeke, Research Bulletin 246, U.S.D.A. Forest Service and the Nebraska College of Agriculture Experiment Station, Lincoln, NB, also available from the Superintendent of Documents.

Viterge News, irregularly published pamphlet on soil nutrition, published by Viterge Farm Services, Inc., Box 16, Kidron, OH 44636.

Small Buildings, Cedar Furniture and Fencing, catalogs and information from Walpole Woodworkers, Inc., Walpole, MA 02081.

White Flower Farm, Litchfield, CT 06759, publishers of the *Garden Book* and *Notes,* which are combination catalog and primer and available for $4/year (or free to regular customers).

Wind Power Digest, Route 2, Box 489, Bristol, IN 46507,

prints information on wind plants, some of which may fit into roof garden plans. Available on a few newsstands for $2/issue or by subscription for $6/4 issues.

Descriptions of Old Apple Varieties in Preservation Orchard, Worcester City Horticultural Society, 30 Elm Street, Worcester, MA 01608.

MAIL-ORDER SEED AND PLANT SOURCES

Blackthorne Gardens, 48 Quincy Street, Holbrook, MA 02343; catalog of hardy Northern plants, $1.

Briar Hills Nurseries, Briarcliff Manor, NY 10510; no catalog but will send snapshots of different topiary designs.

Brimfield Gardens Nursery, 3109 Main Street, Rocky Hill, CT 06067; rare trees, bonsai, landscaping shrubs.

Buell's Greenhouses, Inc., Box 218, Eastford,CT 06242; list of specialty tubers, rhizomes, etc., 25¢ plus a long, self-addressed, stamped envelope.

Burgess Seed & Plant Company, Box 3000, Galesburg, MI 49053; general garden catalog, including some midget vegetables.

Burnett Brothers, Inc., 92 Chambers Street, New York, NY 10007; perennials, grass seed, etc.

W. Atlee Burpee Company, 300 Park Avenue, Warminster, PA 18991; general garden catalog, including a few midget vegetables.

Carroll Gardens, Westminster, MD 21157; rock plants, perennials, wildflowers, and shrubs.

Conard-Pyle Company (Star Roses), West Grove, PA 19390; beautifully illustrated catalog of roses.

Conley's Garden Center, Boothbay Harbor, ME; list of ferns, wildflowers, trees, and shrubs.

DeGiorgi Company, Inc., Council Bluffs, IA 51501; nice, old-fashioned seedbook, including tools, traditional flowers.

DeJager Bulbs, South Hamilton, MA 01982; daffodils, other bulbs, well illustrated.

J. A. Demonchaux Company, Inc., 225 Jackson, Topeka, KS 66603; French vegetable seeds, imported foods.

Edelweiss Gardens, Box 66R, Robbinsville, NJ 08691; orchids, begonias, ferns, trees, and shrubs.

Farmer Seed & Nursery Company, Faribault, MN 55021; general garden catalog.

Far North Gardens, 15621 Auburndale Avenue, Livonia, MI; Barnhaven primroses, wildflower seeds, rock garden plants; clearly written; catalog 25¢.

Ferndale Gardens, 2372 Nursery Lane, Faribault, MN 55021; general garden catalog; tendency to fanciful descriptions, sweepstakes, and giveaways but some interesting specimens and good values.

Gardens of the Blue Ridge, Ashford, NC 28603; bog plants, ferns, perennials, native wildflowers.

Girard Nurseries, Box 428, Geneva, OH 44041; bonsai, broad-leaf evergreens, shrubs; tree seeds.

Glecklers Seedmen, Metamora, OH 43540; unusual vegetables, especially Japanese varieties.

Gurney Seed & Nursery Company, 2683 Page Street, Yankton, SD 57078; outsized general garden catalog, some unusual varieties.

Joseph Harris Company, Inc., Moreton Farm, Rochester, NY 14624; vegetables, flowers, general garden catalog.

The Charles C. Hart Seed Company, Wethersfield, CT 06109; seeds, vegetables, flowers.

Alexander Irving Heimlich, 71 Burlington Street, Woburn, MA 01801; bulbs.

Hemlock Hill Herb Farm, Hemlock Hill Road, Litchfield, CT 06759; herbs, herb plants.

J. I. Hudson, Seedsman, Box 1058, Redwood City, CA 94064; rare seeds; well-written catalog with careful line drawings, 50¢.

Inter-State Nurseries, Hamburg, IA 51644; general catalog.

Jackson & Perkins Company, Medford, OR 97501; good roses.

J. W. Jung Seed Company, Randolph, WI 53956; slightly old-fashioned general garden catalog offering many varieties.

Kelly Brothers Nurseries, Inc., Dansville, NY 14437; general garden catalog.

Joseph J. Kern Rose Nursery, Box 33, Mentor, OH 44060.

Kitazawa Seed Company, 356 West Taylor Street, San Jose, CA 95110; Japanese varieties of vegetables as seeds.

Lakeland Nurseries Sales, Hanover, PA 17331; general garden catalog with a tendency to describe in highblown language, offer sweepstakes and other novelties; have some unusual plants, however.

Lamb Nurseries, East 101 Sharp Avenue, Spokane, WA 99202; hardy perennials, rock plants, herbs.

Henry Leuthardt Nurseries, Inc., East Moriches, NY 11940; dwarf and espalier-trained fruit trees; catalog 25¢.

Mellinger's, 2310 West South Range, North Lima, OH 44452; general garden catalog.

John Messelaar Bulb Company, Inc., Box 269, Ipswich, MA 01938; dahlias, daffodils, gladioli.

Metro Myster Farms, Route 1, Box 285, Northampton, PA 18067; bulbs, vegetables, herbs.

Michigan Bulb Company, 1950 Waldorf N.W., Grand Rapids, MI 49550; bulbs, trees, shrubs.

J. E. Miller Nurseries, Inc., Canandaigua, NY 14424; fruit, berries, nuts; general garden catalog.

Musser Forests, Inc., Indiana, PA 15701; shrubs, trees; well written and illustrated.

The Natural Development Company, Box 215, Bainbridge, PA 17502; seeds, organic plant supplements, cosmetics, etc.

Nichols Garden Nursery, 1190 North Pacific Highway,

Albany, OR 97321; unusual herbs, vegetables, semper-
vivums.

Paradise Gardens, 14 May Street, Whitman, MA 02382;
water plants, accessories, cultural information.

George W. Park Seed Company, Inc., Greenwood, SC
29647; comprehensive general garden catalog; excellent
service.

Peekskill Nurseries, Shrub Oak, NY 10588; ground covers, shrubs.

Pikes Peak Nurseries, RD 1, Penn Run, PA 15765; trees,
shrubs.

Putney Nursery, Inc., Putney, VT 05346; ferns, herbs,
wildflowers.

Rakestraw's Perennial Gardens & Nursery, Burton, MI
48529; rock plants, perennials.

Raraflora, 1195 Stump Road, Feasterville, PA 19047;
rare bonsai, dwarf trees, other specimens.

The Rock Garden, Litchfield, ME 04350; dwarf conifers,
rock plants, shrubs.

Seedway, Inc., Hall, NY 14463; well-laid-out general
catalog.

R. H. Shumway Seedsman, Box 777, Rockford, IL 61101;
wonderful old-fashioned catalog from a general garden
supplier.

Francis M. Sinclair, RFD 1, Route 85, Exeter, NH
03833; hardy native ground covers, ferns, and wildflowers.

Slocum Water Gardens, 1101 Cypress Gardens Road,
Winter Haven, FL 33880; water plants, accessories, cultural information.

Stark Brothers Nurseries & Orchards Company,
Louisiana, MO 63353; fruits and vegetables.

Stern's Nurseries, Geneva, NY 14456; well-illustrated
catalog mostly of fruits and berries with a tendency to
florid prose, 50¢.

Stoke's Seeds, Inc., Box 548, Buffalo, NY 14240; general
garden catalog, including midget vegetables.

Thompson & Morgan, Inc., Box 24, Somerdale, NJ
08083; rare seeds, general garden plants, good information, and some fancy varieties of vegetables.

The Three Laurels, Madison County, Marshall, NC
28753; native wildflowers, ornamental shrubs and trees.

Three Springs Fisheries, Inc., Lilypons, MD 21717;
water plants, fish, accessories, cultural advice; catalog
$1.

William Tricker, Inc., 74 Allendale Avenue, Saddle
River, NJ 07458; water plants, accessories, cultural advice.

Otis Twilley Seed Company, Salisbury, MD 21801;
flower and vegetable seeds, especially Southern specialties.

Van Bourgondien Brothers, Box A, Babylon, NY 11702;
bulbs, flowers, houseplants.

Van Ness Water Gardens, 2460 North Euclid Avenue,
Upland, CA 91786; water plants, accessories, cultural
information; catalog 50¢.

Vick's Wildgardens, Inc., Box 115, Gladwyne, PA
19035; ferns, wildflowers.

Martin Viette Nurseries, Route 25A, East Norwich, NY
11732; excellent catalog of perennials and shrubs available at the nursery only. (Day lilies and pachysandra
sold through the mails.) Catalog 75¢.

The Wayside Gardens Company, Hodges, SC 29695;
general garden catalog—one of the best written and illustrated, more useful than many texts. Excellent variety.

Weston Nurseries, Inc., East Main Street, Hopkintown,
MA 01748; ornamental shrubs, flowers.

White Flower Farm, Litchfield, CT 06759; pay $4/year
(or buy regularly) and get one of the most educational
plant catalogs in print; wide range of high-quality ornamental shrubs, trees, and flowers.

MANUFACTURERS AND DISTRIBUTORS OF GARDEN ACCESSORIES

Many of these companies do not sell direct by mail
but will respond to a request for information by sending
descriptions of their products and a list of retail outlets.
A few also offer free plans or suggestions for using their
products.

Acorn, 1812 Laguna, Santa Barbara, CA 93101. Miniature greenhouses, hydroponics supplies.

Arthur Eames Allgrove, North Wellington, MA 01887.
Wildflowers, terrarium and bonsai supplies.

Anchor Fence Division, Anchor Post Products, Inc.,
6500 Eastern Avenue, Baltimore, MD 21224. Illustrations
of different forms of cyclone fencing; list of distributors.

Arrow Group Industries, 100 Alexander Avenue,
Pompton Plains, NJ 07444. Greenhouses, "growing
dome," and steel sheds.

Ashton, Division of the Ashflash Corporation, 151
Woodward Avenue, South Norwalk, CT 06856. Illustrations of garden tools.

The Atlanta Stove Works, Inc., Atlanta, GA. Cast-iron
garden furniture.

Austin Productions, Inc., 815 Grundy Avenue, Holbrook, NY 11741. Garden sculpture, fountains, some
furniture.

Bartlett Tree Expert Company, 2770 Summer Street,
Stamford, CT 06905. National tree-care service with
offices in many cities.

Dorothy Biddle Service, Hawthorne, NY 10532. Gardening supplies and flower arrangement accessories.

Chapin Watermatics, Inc., 368 North Colorado Avenue,
Watertown, NY 13601. Irrigation systems and equipment.

Colorguard Corporation, 1 Johnson Drive, Raritan, NJ
08869. Colorbond fences—literature and list of distributors.

D-Jay World, 3841 St. Barnabas Road, Silver Hill, MD 20023. Small, propagation-box-sized "greenhouses."

Dayton Bag & Burlap Company, Drawer 8, Dayton, OH 45401. Tubs, plastic mulch materials, wire ties, plastic sheeting for greenhouse windows; greenhouse plans.

Duro-Lite Lamps, Inc., Horticultural Division, 17-10 Willow Street, Fair Lawn, NJ 07410. Vita-Lite, Naturescent, Plant-Lite lamps for winter/indoor gardens.

Earlee, Inc., 726 Spring Street, Jeffersonville, IN 47130. Organic gardening materials by mail.

Ekcin's, Box 643, Concord, NH 03301. Garden tools and books.

Environmental Dynamics, Box 996, Sunnymead, CA 92388. Greenhouses, fertilizers, garden accessories.

Feather Hill Industries, Box 41, Zenda, WI 53195. Window greenhouses, bird feeders.

Featherock, Inc., Box 6190, Burbank, CA 91510. Natural lightweight stone for creating rock gardens on the roof (or even indoors). Instructions for use and list of local distributors.

H. Lawrence Ferguson, Box 5129, Ocean Park Station, Santa Monica, CA 90405. Gardening books—good comprehensive list.

Florentine Craftsmen, 650 First Avenue, New York, NY 10016. Fountains, garden sculpture.

Garden Way Research, Charlotte, VT 05445. Garden books, carts, and cart kits.

General Supplies Company, Box 338, Fallbrook, CA 92028. Hydroponics, greenhouse, and nursery supplies. (Catalog 25¢)

The Green House, 9515 Flower Street, Bellflower, CA 90706. Plant lights, carts, trays, etc.

H. B. H. Industries, Inc., 120 Oregon Avenue, Bronxville, NY 10708. Water-Rite moisture indicators.

Hample Equipment Company, Inc., 1 Miracle Mile, Horseheads, NY 14845. Greenhouses and greenhouse accessories.

Hickory Hollow, Route 1, Box 52, Peterstown, WV 24963. Herb plants, herbal products.

A. H. Hoffman, Inc., Landisville, PA 17538. Organic supplements.

Home Plant Displayers, Inc., 51 East 52 Street, New York, NY 10017. Plant stands, racks, lights.

The House Plant Corner, Ltd., Box 5000, Cambridge, MD 21613. Containers, books, tools, plant foods, etc.

Johns-Manville, Greenwood Plaza, Denver, CO 80217. Irrigation equipment for greenhouses, nurseries, gardens; asphalt tiles, linoleum, indoor-outdoor floor coverings.

Kelly Klosure Systems, Box 1058, Fremont, NB 68025. Greenhouse walls, materials.

Maco, Box 3312, Salem, OR 97302. Greenhouses.

Walt Nicke's Garden Talk, General garden tools, notions and accessories.

Plant Products Corporation, Kennedy Avenue, Blue Point, NY. Fertilizers, list of distributors.

Polymetrics International, Inc., 919 Third Avenue, New York, NY 10022. Plantgard spray-on anti-transpirant for plants during winter, in heavy wind conditions, etc.

Radio Steel & Manufacturing Company, 6515 West Grand Avenue, Chicago, IL 60635. Carts.

Reichhold Chemicals, Inc., Box 81110, Cleveland, OH 44181. Structoglas, translucent, reinforced fiberglass panels for making greenhouses.

Peter Reimuller, the Greenhouseman, Box 2666, Santa Cruz, CA 95063. Greenhouses, including a small model for approximately $100.

Rohm & Haas, Philadelphia, PA 19105. Plexiglas acrylic sheets for making greenhouses, propagation boxes, and other garden equipment.

Roof Manufacturing Company, Pontiac, IL 61764. Carts, mowers.

Rotocrop (USA), Inc., 58 Buttonwood Street, New hope, PA 18938. "Accelerator" compost bin; company suggests that ". . . as there is no anchoring be sure to place it out of the wind and fill it at least ⅓ full immediately" when using it on the roof.

Rough Bros., Box 16010, Cincinnati, OH 45217. Greenhouses and greenhouse furniture.

Seymour-Smith & Son, Inc., Oakville, CT 06779. Pruning tools.

Sudbury Laboratories, Inc., Sudbury, MA 01776. Soil-test kits.

Tube Craft, Inc., 1311 West 80 Street, Cleveland, OH 44012. Plant carts, lights and trays.

Turner Greenhouses, Box 1260, Goldsboro, NC 27530. Greenhouses, greenhouse systems.

Viterge Farm Services, Inc. Box 16, Kidron, OH 44636. Plant foods, soil-test kits.

F. H. Von Damm, 898 Grand Street, Brooklyn, NY 11211. Garden products, fertilizers.

Walpole Woodworkers, Inc., Walpole, MA 02081. Garden furniture, sheds, fencing.

BOTANICAL SOCIETIES AND ASSOCIATIONS

Amateur Rose Hybridizers Association, 5016 Wilkinson Avenue, North Hollywood, CA 91607.

American Association of Nurserymen, 230 Southern Building, Washington, D.C. 20005.

American Begonia Society, 139 North Le Doux Road, Beverly Hills, CA 90211.

American Boxwood Society, Box 85, Boyce, VA 22620.

American Daffodil Society, 89 Chichester Road, New Canaan, CT 06840.

American Dahlia Society, 163 Grant Street, Dover, NJ 07801.

American Fern Society, Department of Botany, University of Rhode Island, Kingston, RI 02881.

American Fuchsia Society, Hall of Flowers, Golden Gate Park, San Francisco, CA 94122.

American Gourd Society, P.O. Box 274, Mt. Gilead, OH 43338.

American Horticultural Society, 910 North Washington Street, Alexandria, VA 22314.

American Iris Society, Missouri Botanical Garden, 2315 Tower Grove Avenue, St. Louis, MO 63110.

American Plant Life Society, P.O. Box 150, LaJolla, CA 92037.

American Pomological Society, c/o L. D. Tukey, 103 Tyson Building, Union Park, PA 16802.

American Rose Society, Box 30,000, Shreveport, LA 71130.

American Society for Horticultural Science, P.O. Box 109, St. Joseph, MI 49085.

Herb Society of America, 300 Massachusetts Avenue, Boston, MA 02115.

Hobby Greenhouse Owners Association of America, 18 Echo, Corte Madera, CA 94925.

Indoor Light Gardening Society of America, Inc., 128 West 58 Street, New York, NY 10019

International Fern Society, 2423 Burritt Avenue, Redondo Beach, CA 90278.

International Geranium Society, 11960 Pascal Avenue, Colton, CA 92324.

International Shade Tree Conference, Box 71, Urbana, IL 61801.

National Chrysanthemum Society, Inc., U.S.A., 394 Central Avenue, Mountainside, NJ 07092.

National Fuchsia Society, 10934 Flory Street, Whittier, CA 90606.

Saratoga Horticultural Foundation, Box 108, Saratoga, CA 95070.

Bibliography

Garden Encyclopedia, Banner Press, Birmingham, AL, 1973 (reprinted U.S. Government publications).

Transit Planting: A Manual, American Horticultural Society, Mount Vernon, VA 22121.

Carleton, R. Milton, *The New Vegetable & Fruit Garden Book*, Henry Regnery Company, Chicago, 1976.

Crandall, Chuck, *Big Plants for Small Budgets—How to Grow Outdoor Plants Indoors*, Chronicle Books, San Francisco, CA, 1974.

Cruso, Thalassa, *Making Things Grow Outdoors*, Alfred A. Knopf, New York, 1973.

Cruso, Thalassa, *Making Vegetables Grow*, Alfred A. Knopf, New York, 1975.

Douglas, James Sholto, *Beginner's Guide to Hydroponics*, Drake Publishers, New York, 1973.

Dupuy, William A., *Our Plant Friends and Foes*, Dover Publications, New York, 1969.

Dworkin, Florence and Stanley, *The Apartment Gardener*, New American Library, New York, 1974.

Edinger, Philip, *Guide to Organic Gardening*, Lane Magazine & Book Company, Menlo Park, CA, 1973 (a Sunset book).

Faust, Joan Lee, *The New York Times Book of Vegetable Gardening*, Quadrangle/The New York Times Book Company, New York, 1975.

Fogg, G. E., *The Growth of Plants*, Penguin Books, London, 1975.

Foster, Catherine Osgood, *The Organic Gardener*, Alfred A. Knopf, New York, 1972.

Harter, Walter, *Organic Gardening for City Dwellers*, Warner Books, New York, 1973.

Hay, Roy and Synge, Patrick M., *The Color Dictionary of Flowers and Plants*, Compact edition, Crown Publishers, New York, 1975.

Heritage, Bill, *The Lotus Book of Water Gardening*, The Hamlyn Publishing Group, Middlesex, England, New York, 1973.

Kraft, Ken and Pat, *Grow Your Own Dwarf Fruit Trees*, Walker Publishing Company, 1974.

Kranz, Frederick H. and Jacqueline L., *Gardening Indoors under Lights*, Lancer Books, New York, 1971.

Langer, Richard W., *The After-Dinner Gardening Book*, The Macmillan Company, New York, 1969.

Loewer, Peter, *The Indoor Water Gardener's How-To-Handbook*, Popular Library, New York, 1973.

Logsden, Gene, *Two-Acre Eden*, Warner Books, New York, 1972.

Mabe, Rex E., *Rooftop and Patio Gardening*, Potpourri Press, P.O. Box 10312, Greensboro, NC 27404, 1974.

Muenscher, Walter Conrad, *Poisonous Plants of the United States*, revised, Collier Books, New York, 1975.

Osborne, Richard, *How to Grow Annuals*, Lane Magazine & Book Company, Menlo Park, CA (a Sunset book).

Petrides, George A., *A Field Guide to Trees and Shrubs*, 2d edition, Houghton Mifflin Company, Boston, 1972 (a Peterson Field Guide).

Pokorny, Jaromir, *A Color Guide to Familiar Trees*, Octopus Books, London, 1974.

Pokorny, Jaromir, *Flowering Shrubs*, Octopus Books, London, 1975.

Powell, Thomas and Betty, *The Avant Gardener*, Houghton Mifflin Company, Boston, 1975.

Riker, Tom and Rottenberg, Harvey, *Food Gardens*, William Morrow & Company, New York, 1975.

Riker, Tom and Rottenberg, Harvey, *The Gardener's Catalog*, William Morrow & Company, New York, 1974.

Robbins, Wilfred W., Weier, T. Elliot, and Stocking, C. Ralph, *Botany, An Introduction to Plant Science*, 3d edition, John Wiley & Sons, New York, 1967.

Robinette, Gary O., *Plants/People/and Environmental Quality*, U.S. Department of the Interior, National

Park Service, Washington, D.C. and American Society of Landscape Architects Foundation.

Seymour, E. L. D., editor, *The Wise Garden Encyclopedia,* Grosset & Dunlap, New York, 1970.

Steffek, Edwin F., *The Pruning Manual,* Van Nostrand Reinhold Company, New York, 1969.

Stone Soup, a Collective, *The Green World: A Guide and Catalog,* Berkley Publishing Corporation, New York, 1975.

Strahler, Arthur N., *Introduction to Physical Geography,* 2d edition, John Wiley & Sons, New York, 1970.

Sunset Editorial Staff, *Basic Gardening Illustrated* (1974); *Gardening in Containers* (1973); *How to Grow Herbs* (1974); *Ideas for Hanging Gardens* (1974); all from Lane Magazine & Book Publishing Company, Menlo Park, CA.

Swann, Lester A. and Papp, Charles S., *The Common Insects of North America,* 1st edition, Harper & Row, New York, 1972.

Taylor, Norman, *The Guide to Garden Shrubs and Trees,* Crown Publishers, 1964.

Taylor, Norman, editor, *Taylor's Encyclopedia of Gardening,* 4th edition, Houghton Mifflin Company, Boston, 1961.

Truex, Philip, *The City Gardener,* Alfred A. Knopf, New York, 1972.

Unwin, Charles W. J., *Unwin's Flowering Bulbs in Colour,* The Hamlyn Publishing Group, Middlesex, England, New York, 1973.

Wentzell, Gail Knight, editor, *How to Grow Bulbs,* revised, Lane Magazine & Book Publishing Company, Menlo Park, CA, 1973.

Westcott, Cynthia, *The Gardener's Bug Book,* 4th edition, Doubleday & Company, New York, 1972.

Williamson, Joseph F., supervising editor, *Pruning Handbook,* Lane Magazine & Book Publishing Company, Menlo Park, CA, 1974.

Yang, Linda, *The Terrace Gardener's Handbook,* Doubleday and Company, New York, 1975.

Zim, Herbert S., editor, *Insect Pests,* Golden Press, New York, 1966.

Index

Page numbers in **boldface** refer to illustrations.